Pia and Simon Pearce

A Way of Living

Photography and design by Glenn Suokko

INTRODUCTION

Pia Pearce

"How's Kevin doing?"

To be honest, that's the question Simon and I have been asked more than any other over the last ten years. Kevin is the youngest of our four sons. On December 31, 2009, at the age of twenty-two, while training as a snowboarder for the 2010 Vancouver Olympics, he sustained a severe traumatic brain injury in Park City, Utah. At that instant, our lives were upended. At first, we weren't sure if Kevin was even going to live through New Year's Eve, and when he did, we started on a journey that has changed our family forever.

Kevin's amazing recovery is one part of what has inspired this revised and expanded edition of *A Way of Living*. In the last ten years so much has changed in our family, in our business, and in our very own way of living; the time seems right to update our story. The original version of this book was first published in October 2009. Three months later, Simon and I moved out west for three months to support Kevin in his recovery. As we faced the scariest and most challenging ordeal of our lives, so many people reached out to share hope and encouragement. For us, the outpouring of support from our loyal customers, employees, family, friends, and many other interested individuals was nothing short of astounding. Now, ten years later, Kevin is doing incredibly well, and we want to invite you into our new book so that we can share more updates.

First, about our family. Our family has always been at the heart of what Simon and I are about since our first son, Andrew, was born in 1981. In the last ten years, we've had three weddings and now have three adorable grandchildren! The table that for so many years was set for six is now set for twelve. We still gather regularly for weekend meals as well as to celebrate holidays and family traditions. Fortunately for us, all four sons and our daughters-in-law have chosen to make their homes in Vermont.

Andrew and Christy were married in 2010. After working with us at Simon Pearce for ten years, Andrew decided to set up his own workshop, Andrew Pearce Bowls, just a short distance from our flagship store and restaurant in Quechee. He now has his own thriving business making beautiful hand-turned wooden bowls, as well as cutting boards and furniture.

Our second son, Adam, gave up his job in order to help Kevin with his rehabilitation during the first and most critical post-injury year. Soon after Kevin returned home to Vermont, renowned movie director Lucy Walker began work on her award-winning HBO documentary, *The Crash Reel*, a compelling story about Kevin and our family as we went through a difficult and transitional time. During the process of making the film, we all became acutely aware of the enormous need for long-term support for people with traumatic brain injury. As a result, Adam and Kevin decided to initiate LoveYourBrain, now a Pearce family foundation. Through the foundation, we work to make a positive difference for those with brain injuries as well as for their caregivers. Adam serves as executive director and his wife, Kyla, as the senior director of the LoveYourBrain Yoga Program. Kevin spreads awareness about LoveYourBrain through his successful career as a motivational speaker. He continues to be personally involved and supportive of the family foundation he helped to create. Together with their team of sixteen, LoveYourBrain is making life-changing impact by creating community where there was isolation, hope where there was despair, and a brighter, healthier future for those whose lives have been so dramatically changed by traumatic brain injuries.

Page 6: Simon and I set a winter holiday table with the glass and pottery our company makes.

Opposite: Our sons, left to right, are Kevin, David, Adam, and Andrew. Each has made his home in Vermont.

Our third son, David, who has Down syndrome, has just celebrated ten years of working with us at our headquarters in Windsor, Vermont. We truly love and appreciate having him participate in the family business. Equally important is that he is a dedicated, reliable, and hard-working employee who considers all his co-workers like family.

Our core values still define us. Our focus on family and our desire to create meaningful work makes us proud. Our loyal customers and friends and the amazing team of people we work with are the ones who make everything possible. A long time ago, I was frequently asked, "Does Simon make all the glass, and do you make all the food?" Anyone who knows us will understand how amusing that question is! In fact, over the past ten years our company has grown considerably and while we still make all our products in the United States, we now have many more people working in all aspects of our business, including the glassblowing started by Simon in Ireland in 1971 and moved by both of us to Vermont in 1981. Our glass is now made in three locations: Quechee and Windsor, Vermont, and Oakland, Maryland. We still make most of the glass exactly the same way as when we started: two skilled craftspeople—a master and a helper—working together, make each piece individually by hand. Our pottery continues to be made at our workshop in Windsor, and our well-known restaurant in Quechee now has a bar that was added in 2013. One of the most profound examples of our way of living is how many amazing people have joined us in our creative endeavors: the 45 individuals working in the glass workshops, 12 in the pottery, and 67 in our kitchen and restaurant are among a total of 281 employees at Simon Pearce. Over the years some people have come, made significant contributions, and then gone on to create their own new way of living. Others have come and stayed with us for five, ten, twenty, and in some cases, thirty years! Each person's impact has been, and continues to be, of great consequence. We couldn't possibly have gotten this far if Simon was making all the glass and I was trying to cook all the food!

Today, even though Simon and I are not (and never were) making everything ourselves, Simon is still very much involved in all facets of the business. He continues to be especially interested in all aspects of design—from glass to glass furnaces to pottery to retail store interiors—as well as in reducing the amount of plastic we use in the company. Our goal is to achieve a greener footprint.

Simon holds our grandson, Bear, Kyla and Adam's son. The kitchen is where our growing family most often gathers for informal conversation, cooking, and sitting down for meals.

In addition to our hydroelectric operation in Quechee, which still generates renewable electricity from the Ottauquechee River, plans are currently underway to install a five-hundred-kilowatt solar array in Windsor. Because our business has, over the last forty years, been so central to our "way of living," there isn't anything about it we don't deeply care about. What was once a very small workshop with five people at the end of a *boreen* in Ireland is now a thriving enterprise where many more people join us in creating something that is still remarkably unique. We are one of the few companies left in the world that still makes high-quality clear glass by hand.

My own life continues to be happily intertwined with Simon's and that of our sons and their families. We both serve on the Simon Pearce board of directors and work closely with our chief executive officer, Jay Benson. Especially rewarding is the time I spend working with the wonderful team that supports David, allowing him to live in his own home as well as be gainfully employed. Being an educational advocate for my grandchildren is another very fulfilling part of my life as is my role as board member and president of LoveYourBrain. Having the flexibility to follow these many varied interests is truly a great joy rivaled only by the opportunity to spend as much time as possible with our adorable grandchildren!

Our revised and expanded edition of *A Way of Living* is our opportunity to update you about what's changed at the company and in our family over the last ten years: the stories are revised to more accurately reflect where we are today, there are hundreds of beautiful photographs by Glenn Suokko of new glass and pottery designs pictured in our home as well as images he took in our workshops in Quechee and Windsor, and we've included eighteen delicious new recipes that reflect the evolving tastes of Vermont at our restaurant. Here, you'll see what our growing family looks like now and how we've evolved over the last decade.

Finally, and most importantly, I want to acknowledge our loyal, dedicated, and incredibly supportive customers, friends, and family. You are the ones who have made it possible for this vision of ours—our way of living—to come true! Thank you for always standing behind us and for appreciating what we do. Your feedback, requests, and critical insights have helped us become who and what we are today. Your concern for our family, and especially for Kevin, means more to Simon and me than we could ever possibly express.

Opposite: Hartland stemware, like many Simon Pearce designs, is named after a Vermont town. Hartland is one of Simon's earliest designs after his move from Ireland to Vermont.

Following page: Simon blows glass at the Windsor workshop.

OUR GLASS AND POTTERY

Simon Pearce

As a young boy growing up in Shanagarry, Ireland, I enjoyed working in my father's pottery, which was located in the stable and courtyard next to our house. My responsibilities involved preparing the clay, making and glazing the pots, and packing the pots in the kiln. Because I enjoyed making things and learned more from experience than from the classroom, I left school when I was sixteen. My parents were supportive and encouraged me to apprentice with Harry Davis, a well-known English potter who had left Cornwall, England, to set up a pottery studio in Nelson, New Zealand. From Liverpool, I set out on a cargo ship and sailed to the other side of the world. I worked for two years with Harry and learned everything I could from the master potter.

I was also inspired by my godfather, Patrick Scott, a well-known Irish painter, and in particular by the collection of old Georgian glass that he and his partner had collected for many years. I soon developed an interest in glass, and my work and life took a turn. Much like my parents, who were always looking out for early pottery, I enjoyed going to small antique shops and weekend flea markets to look for old Georgian glass, which was blown and made by hand in the eighteenth and nineteenth centuries. I started collecting it, wanting to learn more about it and how to make glass like it. It was the simplicity and individuality of old glass and the difference between it and what was being made commercially at the time that I found fascinating. In comparison to mass-produced glass, old glass—handmade and finished one piece at a time by a craftsman rather than a machine—had character and uniqueness. The old glassmaking processes were unlike the mass-production techniques that were introduced during the Industrial Revolution. Although the idea of making glass by hand in the 1960s was an anachronism, it appealed to me nevertheless. I was curious to find out whether hand-finished glass—like the old glass I liked—could be made economically on a small scale.

My quest to learn traditional glassblowing skills began in the late 1960s and proved to be an enormous challenge and a lengthy journey, one that took me far from home. My goal was to learn anything and everything I could about glass and furnace technology, and then adapt that knowledge to create a small workshop for making clear glass—stemware and glasses, bowls, and pitchers—for everyday use.

I first wrote to many companies, asking to meet with their glassmakers, wanting to learn from them, but for all my enthusiasm and genuine interest, most of them either didn't respond or turned me down; the glass factories in Ireland and England were very protective of their processes. I then went to the Royal College of Art in London—the only school in England at the time that had a glass department—but it was mostly limited to studies in making one-of-a-kind art glass, and it offered little instruction about the skills needed for making functional glassware. While in London, I practiced in the evenings at glassmaker Sam Herman's studio, the Glasshouse, in Covent Garden. After a year, I went to Amsterdam to the Gerrit Rietveld Academie, which also had a glass department, but I soon discovered that I couldn't progress any further; the academy's educational focus was once again on art glass, not functional glass. A professor at the academy introduced me to some glassmakers at the Leerdam factory, an hour's drive outside Amsterdam. It was here that I finally experienced the inner workings of a real glass factory. I was hired as an assistant to the factory's top glassmaker. Although we didn't speak the same language—

Today, I can occasionally be found in the glass workshop trying out new ideas for designs, or simply making glass, as shown here, where I'm creating a smaller variation of my Essex design.

he couldn't speak a word of English and I couldn't speak a word of Dutch—we worked together for three months, making glass. I made notes and learned a lot, but I didn't actually get to blow glass or finish it myself. From the Netherlands, I moved on to Venini, a highly revered glass factory on the island of Murano in Venice, Italy, where I again worked for three months as a helper. The opportunity to observe glassblowing at one of the greatest glass factories in Europe turned out to be an extraordinary experience, but I was still an observer, not a glassmaker. In 1969, I left Italy and went on to Scandinavia.

In Scandinavia, glassmaking at last started to make sense. I arrived in Denmark and went to Kastrup-Holmegaard, where the management was very open, encouraging me to set up my own workbench and start experimenting with and making glass. From Denmark, I drove to Orrefors Glass, a factory deep in the forest in the Småland region of Sweden, where, during an earlier time, there had been dozens of glass factories, and the trees from the thick forest had been used to fuel the glass-melting furnaces. I became a student in the factory, and for six months I learned about technique, experimented with design, and made samples of the kind of glass I hoped to be able to make in my own workshop one day. During vacation periods at Orrefors, I worked at two more factories in Sweden—Sandvik and Boda—before heading back to Ireland in 1970 to build my first workshop.

In Ireland, I spent almost a year building a glass studio and workshop store next to my home in Bennettsbridge, County Kilkenny. With the help of three apprentices, I finally started making my own glass in 1971. The early years at my glass studio were especially challenging, and I didn't have the technical expertise necessary to accomplish all that was essential for making a successful business. Although it was often difficult, I persevered, and through trial and error I developed a small furnace that could produce the high-quality clear glass I was determined to make.

In 1973, I opened my first retail store in the village of Clifden on the west coast of Ireland, not far from Galway. Customers appreciated the character and integrity of my glassware, and sales soon increased. In the mid-1970s, I expanded the retail business, opening two more stores: one in Dublin and another in Kenmare, County Kerry.

Attached to the end of the glassblower's pontil, the glass is heated in a small furnace. Timing is critical, and the glass must remain hot while the craftsman is working it. The pontil leaves a mark in the base of the piece being worked, where the tool is released from the glass. Some glassmakers choose to eliminate the pontil mark, but years ago I decided to leave it on the bottom of each of our pieces, just as glassmakers had done hundreds of years ago.

Opposite: The Essex wine glass (originally called the Round wine glass) is one of the first glasses I designed and produced in Ireland. It has remained a popular glass due to its versatility, and it continues to be produced today in our glassblowing workshop in Quechee. Essex represented everything that was essential to my vision when it came to weight, size, and proportions.

Following pages: Most of our stemware is made in Quechee. Here, glass master David Weiland-Alter, who has been working with us since 1987, makes a Woodstock Balloon wine glass.

Patricia (Pia) McDonnell and I met in 1977 while I was visiting some friends in the United States. Two years later, we were married in her hometown. Pia grew up in Peapack, New Jersey, a beautiful little town an hour west of New York City. Having just completed her doctoral dissertation in education at the University of San Francisco, Pia knew a great deal about education but almost nothing about the glass business. However, she had a very easy time talking with many of the visitors who found their way down the long lane to our glass studio in Bennettsbridge. Observing that many of the visiting Americans truly appreciated the glass we were making and would be interested in purchasing more of our products back home, Pia developed a mail-order catalogue and sales increased. Even though Ireland had been very good to us, Pia and I eventually decided to move closer to her family and take advantage of the exciting opportunities available in the United States.

Our plan was to establish a traditional glassblowing factory and retail store on the East Coast of the United States. We looked at several sites along Hudson River tributaries in New York State, but something was always lacking. Our search continued until we drove to the small Vermont village of Quechee to look at a two-hundred-year-old former woolen mill. When we arrived and saw the old brick building, the majestic river, and the water falling over the dam, we knew it was right. It had everything we were looking for: a beautiful setting to live and work in, a fantastic workspace with enough room for a retail store, and the potential for harnessing natural energy and converting the river's power into electricity to fuel our glass furnace. I had given considerable thought to the possibilities of hydropower: an alternative, local source of energy could make sense both economically and environmentally.

Our assumptions were right about what we could make of the mill, and our perseverance and dedication to the craft we loved guided us forward. I built a glass furnace and made glass with glassblowers P. J. Skehan, Patrick Kelly, and Charles Shackleton; all three had moved from Bennettsbridge to join us in Vermont. Pia ran a small retail store in the front lobby where she sold our first American-made products.

Because I have always had a strong affection for simple, well-designed tableware, early on we developed a pottery at the mill with the careful guidance of master potter Miranda

Opposite: I no longer blow glass as much as I did years ago, but I now look forward to occasionally working alongside our team of glassblowers at our workshop in Windsor.

Following pages: Master glassblower Jake Cole (left) and assistant Jeremy Bastille (right) work together to make a large Nantucket Hurricane.

Our glass is handcrafted by artisans who have trained for years to acquire the skills necessary to achieve the high quality of glassware we make. In our workshops, glassblowers work in teams of two to create one piece of glass at a time. This process gives each piece of glass its own distinctive character. We continue the educational tradition of master and apprentice. Apprenticeships last at least two years, and it can take three to six years—or longer—to become a master glassblower. Glassblowing is intense work that requires great skill and concentration. Some of our master craftsmen have been making glass and training apprentices in our workshops for ten to twenty years. Our glassblowers, like all the individuals who work with us, become an important part of the Simon Pearce family.

Thomas. To complement our glassware, we continue to design and produce extensive lines of dinnerware that remain faithful to our tradition of simplicity. We also carefully select and offer tabletop products such as wooden bowls and cutting boards, placemats, napkins, and flatware to harmonize with our own handcrafted products. In essence, we offer customers a variety of options for creating beautiful tables where all elements are compatible.

Now, thirty-eight years since we settled in Vermont, we have a vibrant company of 281 employees; 45 glassblowers and 12 potters create beautiful, innovative pieces with the quality, distinctiveness, character, and feeling I had always sought in our handmade glass and pottery. We now make glass in three locations: in addition to our first facility at the mill in Quechee, we built a facility in nearby Windsor, Vermont, in 1993; and we bought a facility in Mountain Lake Park, Maryland, in 1999. All our pottery is made in Windsor. We sell our products at our own retail stores, online, and through our print catalogue and a network of fine retailers across the country.

Pia and I wanted to create a full experience for the many visitors who are interested in our work and make our facilities their destination. We established a restaurant at our flagship store in Quechee to offer diners a nice meal made from fresh, local Vermont ingredients and the opportunity to experience our products firsthand by drinking from our glassware and eating from our dinnerware. At the same locations, guests can visit our stores and watch craftsmen blow glass at our workshops.

Years ago, my goal was to renew the art of glassblowing in an era when virtually all glass was mass-produced and manufactured by assembly-line production based on speed and uniformity. Today I find that many people appreciate the special, unique kind of glass I was drawn to at an early age. At Simon Pearce, we choose to carry on the tradition of blowing and finishing glass by hand, one piece at a time. The techniques used in our workshops are essentially the same as those that were used in Europe hundreds of years ago. While remaining true to these time-honored methods, we have worked to build a business capable of sustaining a consistently high level of quality and production, proving that handmade products can compete in today's marketplace.

Our customers often tell us that they choose our products

Our pottery facility in Windsor, Vermont, is an active operation where skilled craftspeople produce several different ranges of dinnerware and a large selection of bowls, vases, lamps, and pitchers in a variety of colors. Our ceramic products, made of a high-quality vitrified stoneware, go through multiple hand processes and are made one piece at a time, utilizing a combination of traditional hand-thrown and contemporary methods. After a pot is formed and dried, it is ready for the first of its two firings. The bisque kiln, packed with an average of eight hundred pots, reaches 1,850°F over a twelve-hour period; through this low-temperature firing, moisture is taken out of the pots. After the kiln has cooled, the pots are removed, hand-dipped in liquid glaze to create crackled or non-crackled finishes, and fired again, this time at a much higher temperature of 2,350°F. From start to finish, each of our pottery products takes approximately three weeks to complete. Our pottery is created to complement our glass at the table. Shown here are Mike Trempe (top), who has been working with us since 1997, and Jeff Rogers (below), who started in 2017.

for themselves and for others to mark all sorts of memorable occasions in a special way. We hope our customers feel a connection to us and all the individuals who work at our company by understanding and appreciating the inherent artisanship in creating classic products that will stand the test of time. Making beautiful products of unmatched quality and versatility that can be used every day is paramount to our work.

In the early years, I blew glass most days, but for many years I have been so involved with managing and building our company that I haven't had time to blow glass—until recently. I have always designed our products, and in the last several years, James Murray, a talented designer, has been working with me to create new forms and has designed many of his own, including some of our Pure Collection and the popular Echo Lake line. One person in our company combines a multitude of exceptional skills and understands the entire technical process of glassmaking: Jan Mollmark, a great production manager and engineer, who came to us from Sweden twenty-five years ago. Jan has an amazing ability to implement our ideas and make things happen. Our remarkable collaboration is an important factor in our company's expansion over the years.

Input from my family on product design—especially from Pia—has always been important to me. Our four sons have grown up and witnessed the growth of our family business, and they have been keenly interested in and a critical part of everything we do at Simon Pearce. Pia provides a family update in her introduction to this book.

In 2016, Rizzoli International Publications published *Design for Living*, a book I collaborated on with Glenn Suokko, that tells the story of my journey as a glassblower and glass designer, tracing my path and inspirations from Ireland to Vermont.

Recently, I made some changes to my daily routine. Now, I spend most mornings collaborating with our chief executive officer, Jay Benson, or reviewing designs with James Murray, senior vice president of design and product development. Occasionally, I blow glass alongside our glassblowers at our workshop in Windsor, and every week I stay connected with many employees in all parts of the company.

A wide variety of our pottery after the bisque-kiln firing but before the pots are glazed and refired in the kiln.

Opposite: Our eldest son, Andrew, opened his own workshop to make wooden bowls in Hartland, Vermont, just a few miles from our glass workshop and restaurant in Quechee.

Above: Andrew's Live Edge Bowls rest on top of an old Tudor chest and below a shelf of some of my glass designed and made over many years.

OUR HOME, TABLE, AND COOKING

Pia Pearce

Our home is not only a house; it is the place where Simon and I provide a sense of warmth, comfort, safety, and stability for our family, as well as a place for us all to be creative, innovative, and imaginative. The location of our home is as important as the structure we call a house. I have learned that making conscious choices about how to live and what to live with offers abundant possibilities for an interesting and satisfying life.

Simon and I grew up in rural settings—Simon in Shanagarry, a small town on the southern coast of Ireland, and I in a beautiful valley in rural New Jersey. The natural environments we were raised in not only made strong impressions on us, but have influenced us throughout our lives: for Simon, an ancient bog and the coast of the powerful Atlantic Ocean; for me, the protected agrarian landscape, woods, and streams where I played with my eight siblings and friends.

Simon's parents, Lucy and Philip, and mine, Peggy and Murray, cared a great deal about where they lived, their homes, and the furnishings and objects they chose to live with. The open countryside we each grew up in suited Simon as it did me, and the experiences and memories of our childhood homes later informed

us when we began to design and make our home together in Vermont. When we were married in September 1979, we decided to live in the quietude of country; first in Bennettsbridge, County Kilkenny, Ireland, in an old stone farmhouse that Simon was renovating at the end of a very long country lane, and later, in 1985, in Vermont, where we decided to set our house a considerable distance from the nearest road.

In designing our house in Vermont, Simon and I made critical choices about its integration into the landscape, the design of the buildings, what to live with, and what to leave out. Our home reflects our combined interest in creating a simple experience in a beautiful setting that allows us to foster creativity. The functionality of the land, buildings, and gardens and the importance of the household items and artwork we have collected and find meaningful inspire us in our work. The design of everything within our view and reach—from the largest outdoor spaces to the glass we put on our table—is important to us.

Simon and I made a conscious decision to make the first floor of the barn we renovated for our home into one big room so that our entire family could essentially always be together. There is an openness and volume to the space that we find liberating. We wanted the room to feel old and at the same time contemporary. The idea of timelessness appeals to us. We furnished the room with antique wooden country furniture from Ireland and Vermont, contemporary furniture, objects we have collected, and our own glass and pottery. The large, comfortable room serves as kitchen, dining room, and sitting room.

We designed our house to be used and enjoyed and, more than anything, as a place that would function well for our four active, energetic boys when they were young. We built the house when our eldest son, Andrew, was four. Our youngest, Kevin, is now thirty-one. The house itself is unquestionably informal; its personality reflects the casual manner in which we like to live. The design is clean and clear; the furnishings, comfortable. Our home contains many meaningful objects that Simon, his brother Stephen, or other craftsmen we know have made. And a simple or rich story of its maker exists in each of the unique pieces.

Our collection of glass, pottery, and art suggests our appreciation for what we consider good, simple design. Simon freely admits that he is not a serious collector, nor an artist, but the objects and artwork we have chosen to live with offer clues to

Pages 34 and 36: Our house itself consists of two buildings. The first building is an old barn frame that we purchased, disassembled, moved, and rebuilt to create an open-plan house for ourselves and our four young sons. Later, we added a brick wing that has the feeling and look of an old Irish country house.

Page 37: We designed our pool house to be reminiscent of the small stone buildings in Ireland, where Simon was raised.

Page 38: The house is composed of two buildings connected by a brick- and glass-walled passageway.

Page 39: The gardening season in Vermont is short, but we enjoy watching our garden change throughout the entire year. In summer, the garden also provides a wonderful place for outdoor dining.

Opposite: Our open kitchen and dining area serves as a place to relax and enjoy the company of friends and our growing family.

his personal development as a designer. Simon's collection of old Georgian glass is extensive; his collection of pottery distinctive and personal; and our collection of art spiritual. What all the objects in our house have in common is our interest in their utility, design, form, materials, color, and expression.

Living with attractive functional objects is important to us and inspires us to use them every day. Our goal has always been to make beautiful glass that can be used regularly. Simon, through creative process and technical innovation, was able to unite timeless design, character, and function in glassware that can be used meal after meal. And because of his early experience and ongoing interest in pottery, we developed dinnerware with the same pragmatism and aesthetic goals. Living with and using beautiful things at home makes every day of the week much richer.

The possibilities when making choices for the table and what is placed on it are what make table settings interesting. Our table is an important expression of who we are. Although good food and the right tableware provide the best starting point for an enjoyable meal, it is the individuals who gather around the table, and their conversations, that make the meal memorable.

In Ireland, when Simon was a boy, the kitchen table was the heart of the Pearce family. Simon's mother Lucy, father Philip, brother Stephen, sister Sarah, and he would gather around the table for three meals a day, every day. It was the place where they shared stories and experiences. The Pearce family business, Shanagarry Pottery, and its handmade products reflected the important things going on in the lives of each family member, and they spoke about them when they gathered around the table. Simon, our sons, and I regularly have the same kinds of conversations about our glass and tableware when we gather at our table in Vermont.

When I was a young girl in New Jersey, breakfast was one of the more important rites of the day. Our breakfast room—the place where nine children gathered punctually to eat before setting off for school—was where our day began. Each evening we gathered for dinner in the dining room, where my mother always set a beautiful table. In my childhood home, the table was also a place for celebration. Giving toasts on special occasions was a tradition that has been passed down in our family for many generations. On holidays it was—and still is—an opportunity to speak personally to those gathered around the table about things that one might not ordinarily share at other times.

Page 42: Our comfortable kitchen dining table and chairs were made by Charles Shackleton who came from Ireland to settle in Vermont.

Page 43: Although their countries of origin can often be identified, much of the old glass in our collection is anonymous. The glass was made by artisans, and more often than not was not signed by the maker.

Opposite: Among our paintings are works by Simon's godfather, Irish artist Patrick Scott. Scott is widely known for his extensive series of paintings using gold leaf on linen. These meditative paintings are characterized by and reflective of his interest in Buddhism and are particularly appreciated for their deep and calm simplicity.

Above: The Warren bud vase, alongside Burlington pottery in Moss Glen, one of our recent pottery designs. Opposite: Burlington pottery with a lovely dessert from our restaurant alongside our Westport flatware and Simon's one-of-a-kind bud vase and glasses.

Good design, natural materials, and timelessness are important to Simon and me. The tables in our house are solid and made of wood, and in some cases, slate. Most of our tables are old country pieces, but a few are new, such as those by our friend, furniture maker Charles Shackleton. The wooden chairs around the tables possess quiet but sturdy personalities. Durability and comfort are critical; we like to linger at the table. Like our collection of unique pieces of old glass, the variety of chairs in our house is more like a family of individuals than a complete matching set. And there is always enough room to pull up another chair.

Oftentimes we set our table with a variety of glassware and dinnerware. Because the design expression of our own glass and pottery is so consistent, the informal mix becomes whole, yet varied—a subtle blend of similar differences. We frequently mix some of Simon's earliest stemware and pottery with some of his newer designs. And we often integrate other objects made by craftsmen we know personally or whose works we have collected. Our choice is to live with things that have connections to the individuals who made them; they bring life and stories to our table because of our appreciation for the makers, their work, and skill. Conversation about the tableware is inevitable because the objects themselves are compelling and alive with personality, history, and significance.

The creative value inherent in choosing to live with old and new, well-made, beautifully designed, functional objects inspires our work in glass and pottery. By making and offering our own glass and pottery products, we hope to be part of a continuum in passing on our interests to others who share a similar appreciation of timeless design—interests that cultivate a desire to create and live in a place that is innovative and interesting.

When it comes to food at our table, there is nothing more satisfying than cultivating a garden and cooking with the harvest from it. Reflecting on the roots of our interest in good food, Simon and I again turn to our early familial experiences. My mother, a superb cook, has always enjoyed the entire process of providing wonderful meals for her family and friends. She loves entertaining and has earned herself a fine reputation for hosting imaginative dinner parties where her guests can always count on the meals she serves to be creative, interesting, and satisfying. How the table looks and how it is set are very important to her. Resplendent as the atmosphere she creates, my mother has always been interested

Opposite: A kitchen shelf in our home is organized with some of our collection of glass and pottery—a collection that has slowly grown over thirty-eight years.

Page 50: Years ago, in Ireland, Simon's mother discovered a heavy blue-and-white wool fabric that was used as a horse blanket. She liked its design and sought out its maker, Kerry Woolen Mills, and ordered yards of it to use in making curtains for her house. I fell in love with the idea, too, and ordered bolts of the same wool to be shipped to Vermont, where we had curtains of it made for our house. The heavy wool makes sense in winter when we draw the curtains to keep the house warm.

Page 51: An antique Irish dresser in our kitchen is filled with an assortment of Simon Pearce glass.

Above: An Andrew Pearce bowl rests on an antique Irish cupboard. Opposite: Simon's Nantucket Hurricanes keep company with an old hurricane he found in an antique shop.

in simple, good cooking. With care and thoughtfulness, she uses fresh ingredients and prepares food for the table in a straightforward yet innovative way. She also enjoys teaching other people how to cook, and I learned the most important lessons of cooking from her, just as she learned how to cook from her mother. Growing up in a family of nine children, I appreciated that mealtime was not only about eating but also, and more importantly, about being together.

Simon remembers that his mother loved to cook as well. She was a fantastic cook who used fresh ingredients from her garden, which she tended herself. She developed great relationships with the local vendors who in those days delivered meat and fish to the back door of the Pearce house. They talked of local news, and they talked of cuts of meat; she loved to cook stews and casseroles. Simon hunted quite a bit—duck, pheasant, and rabbit—and his mother prepared and made wonderful dishes from the game he brought home for her to cook.

Today we toss convention aside to create a new experience in our kitchen. In our house, especially when our four sons, three daughters-in-law, and three grandchildren are visiting, we might make a few different meals at the same time. This is antithetical to earlier traditions, when I—like Simon's mother and mine—provided one meal and everyone ate the same thing at the same time. On particular holidays, of course, we still prepare the singular, much-appreciated Thanksgiving turkey or the Christmas roast, half-fearing that no one would come home if we didn't. But today, whoever happens to be at home helps prepare the food and cook it. Everyone provides input on what they wish to prepare and offers to help others with what they are making. The benefit of our non-traditional manner is that we each have what we wish to eat when we sit down. The process is informal but important—our family loves good food and gathering together to enjoy it. Cooking as a family provides an opportunity to work together and to create wonderful and satisfying meals. We all pitch in and bring our own interests and style in cuisine and presentation to the table. Variation is constant, and learning about what someone else in the kitchen is preparing is rewarding to the group. Having an assortment of Simon Pearce glassware and tableware to serve with makes a distinctive presentation. Often Simon likes to bring home new glass or pottery to hear what we think about the designs. We value discussing tableware while we are using it because we want

Simon's mother, Lucy, made a loaf of brown bread in her kitchen in Shanagarry, Ireland, and brought it to the Allen family at Ballymaloe House, a country-house hotel nearby. The Allens, stunned by its flavor, began to make it at Ballymaloe's famous restaurant and have served it there ever since. When we brought the recipe to our restaurant in Vermont, we gave it the Ballymaloe name. See pages 108-9 for the recipe.

Simon and I do a fair amount of entertaining in our home and it is a joy to set our tables for guests with the glass and pottery our company makes. Shown here, I set a table for six with our Hartland goblets and wine glasses, and Hartland candlesticks. In our Cavendish cereal bowls, I served a butternut squash soup, which our restaurant serves in-season. On the Cavendish dinner plate, I served a rendition of our restaurant's Roasted Heirloom Carrots (see recipe on pages 156–57). The flatware is Westport. An Andrew Pearce wood serving platter is filled with Rory's Irish Scones from our restaurant (see pages 110–11 for the recipe).

to make sure our products are the best they can be before we offer them to our customers.

Another tradition we maintain in our home is somewhat akin to saying grace or prayers before a meal, and it reflects our consideration of mindfulness practice. When everyone is seated, we observe a moment of silence. One person at the table then strikes a small, half-dome-shaped brass bell with a small wooden rod. While the bell is ringing, the clear, strong sound waves reverberate into the air, and then slowly diminish into silence. For us, the event, which stems from our interest in Buddhist practices, is simple; the sound is spiritual, and the result is calming. Focusing on the sound of the bell allows us to become conscious of the present moment.

The appreciation Simon and I have for creating a comfortable home, interesting tables, and cooking fresh food began in our childhoods. Each of our parents set good examples of living simply and well. Simon and I value the thoughtful preparation of good food, the use of attractive dinnerware, and making functional glass and ceramics for the table. We have tried to raise our sons to embrace the qualities of mindfulness and creativity that have guided our way of living. Enjoying the good company of family and friends and the rewarding conversation that often happens at our table brings meaning and joy to our lives.

Glass has the natural capacity to engage light and make a table inviting and festive. Shown here are our Hartland stem candlesticks and Woodstock tumblers.

Once a year, as many family members as can come gather in our kitchen to make large batches of tomato chutney. There are several ingredients to chop, so the more hands, the better! The chutney was a staple in Simon's house in Ireland, and his mother loved making it as much as her family loved eating it. Our own four boys grew up loving it, and now our daughters-in-law and our grandchildren seem to love it just as much (see the recipe on pages 106–7).

Opposite: In the kitchen with Simon, Adam, and Kevin.

Following pages: With our grandson Oliver and Andrew; our granddaughter, Madison, and Kevin.

Above: Our daughter-in-law Kyla holds her and Adam's son, Bear, at a family gathering.

Opposite: Our granddaughter, Madison, helps her father, Andrew, light a candle in one of Simon's early hurricanes that is no longer being made.

Previous four pages, this page, and opposite: At our home, family gatherings are often informal. We like to put aside the idea of matched table settings to create a unique presentation. We often set our table with a variety of our glassware and dinnerware, as well as products made by friends and fellow craftspeople. Around the table shown on this page are Oliver, Andrew, and Christy; on the opposite page: Kevin, Oliver, David, Madison, me, Simon, and Adam.

Kevin and his wife, Kaitlyn (Ford) Pearce, outside the Mill in Quechee.

Opposite: The glass Pumpkins and Echo Lake Hurricanes were designed by Simon Pearce's vice president of design and product development, James Murray.

Previous pages: In a quiet moment, Simon's recently redesigned Stratton wine glasses pair well with a Nantucket Hurricane.

A table set for friends in our kitchen includes a wonderful Pecan Tart from our restaurant. See pages 180–81 for the recipe.

Above and opposite: Late afternoon dessert time. See pages 186–87 for the recipe for our restaurant's popular Maple Crème Brûlée.

Opposite: A Providence centerpiece from our PURE Collection—unique works of art in glass—rests upon a wooden table by Andrew Pearce.

Above and following pages: When it comes to style, Simon has always preferred simplicity and versatility. His design ethos can be seen in his Woodstock white wine glasses and tumblers.

Above: Made for us in California, our four Simon Pearce reserve wines—Pinot Noir, Chardonnay, Blanc de Noir, and Cabernet Sauvignon—are offered at our restaurant in Quechee and can also be purchased at the Simon Pearce Quechee and Windsor retail stores.

Opposite: The clarity of our glass reflects the warm glow of candlelight.

Opposite and above: One of Simon's most innovative designs, our Woodbury bowl shows its contents to dramatic effect.

Following pages: Our Vermont Evergreens are very challenging to produce. Each tree consists of one to three gathers of glass, each placed on top of the other. While the glass is hot, it is cut with shears and shaped, making each tree truly unique, just as in nature.

Opposite and above: Around the winter holidays, we like to decorate using our Vermont Evergreens, which recently have been made in different styles such as bubbles, silver leaf, or snowy branches. Adding our Polar Bears to these festive, nature-inspired vignettes brings the winter indoors.

Opposite and above: We love candlelight. The darkness of winter is an especially important time when we light the candles in our many candle holders and hurricanes and watch the dazzling, festive glow of glass and all its reflections brighten the short days and long nights.

When spring arrives in Vermont and the gardens unfurl, we can never have enough vases on hand. Page 94: Simon made a few one-of-a-kind bud vases for Mother's Day gifts. Page 95: Our vases are perfect for arranging branches. Above: The Barre bud vase is perfect for all sorts of sweet garden picks. Opposite: Our extra-large Woodbury vase stands tall and strong, allowing full and dramatic arrangements during all times of the year.

RECIPES FROM OUR RESTAURANT

Pia Pearce

When Simon and I bought the mill in Quechee in 1980, we originally planned to serve coffee, scones, and brown bread at small tables around a big, open fireplace, but we eventually realized that serving lunch might make more sense. In 1983 we opened a small restaurant and offered a basic, nutritious luncheon menu of soups, quiche, and salad—and that was the extent of the menu. But since we had a kitchen and a license to prepare and sell food, we soon decided to expand our offerings and serve dinner. Running a glass business, a pottery, and a restaurant proved to be more challenging than we had anticipated, and at one point in 1984 we were almost ready to close the restaurant. But several members of my family, along with some devoted friends, wanted to ensure the restaurant's survival, so they arrived in Quechee to help us stay open during a busy Labor Day weekend. My brothers Stephen and Andrew took turns tending the bar, sister Anna served the drinks, and sister Peg waited on tables while her husband, Cy Vance, alternately washed dishes and greeted guests as they arrived at the door. My mother, Peggy, took charge of cooking in the kitchen. It was a magical moment, and their enthusiasm and support convinced us to persevere, to bring our restaurant to another level. As a result, we hired a good manager and chef, and these two critical positions helped pave the way for a successful business.

When people dine at our restaurant in Quechee, they enjoy the simple good food it offers in a relaxed setting overlooking a stunning river, an impressive waterfall, and a charming wooden covered bridge. The wholesome style of cuisine and simple presentation at the tables reflect our ideal of timeless unfussy quality.

Our restaurant's executive chef, Jeremy Conway, wants to make sure that our guests receive the best-quality food possible. With input from Simon, me, and our restaurant director, Jerod Rockwell, Jeremy changes the menu to coincide with the four distinct seasons in New England to provide patrons with a taste of what is harvested in Vermont. He is able to obtain the best in-season produce by working with several local farmers, who supply the kitchen with almost all its vegetables and salad greens during the warmer months of the year. The quality of the food served is inherent in the taste of greens and vegetables that were picked that morning; the thick, rich cream that arrived fresh from the farm that day; or the savory chicken that was raised free-range that season. The restaurant is proud to support its local farmers and has developed longstanding support from regional partners such as Crossroad Farm, McNamara Dairy, Blue Moon Sorbet, Vermont Artisan Coffee and Tea, Vermont Creamery, Strafford Organic Creamery, Putney Mountain Winery, Cabot Creamery, Northeast Family Farms, Wood Mountain Fish, and many more. The bar at the restaurant features beers by dozens of Vermont's most well-known craft breweries and selections from some of Vermont's finest distilleries.

Many diners have asked about our recipes and providing them to those who share a culinary passion is an honor. Several recipes included in this book have roots in Ireland while a few originated in the Pearce family, and many come from our restaurant kitchen in Quechee. Because the recipes were intended for our restaurant, where we serve many guests, they have been adapted to work well for those who are cooking for a family or planning a dinner party at home; much of the preparation can be done ahead of time and many of the dishes can be assembled and finished right before guests arrive. Some of the recipes benefit from being started a day ahead of serving time. For a complete list of recipes organized by page number and course, see page 105.

Page 98: When we moved from Ireland to Vermont, the Mill in Quechee is where Simon and I lived, worked, and opened a restaraunt. The dining room at our restaurant in Quechee cantilevers over the Ottauquechee River, providing guests with a view of the waterfall and one of Vermont's prettiest covered bridges.

Opposite and pages 102-103: The atmosphere shifts from day to night at our restaurant in Quechee. Every evening, the wooden tables are set with white tablecloths, and romantic, flickering light glows from our many candle holders.

THE RECIPES

Opposite: Standing with me in my home kitchen during one of our recipe tastings are Jerod Rockwell, restaurant director, and Jeremy Conway, executive chef.

Pearce Family Tomato Chutney

Makes 7 pints

7 to 8 pounds ripe tomatoes, peeled, cored, and chopped

1 pound yellow onions, chopped

4 cloves garlic, minced

3 or 4 apples, peeled, cored, and chopped

2 to 3 pounds dark brown sugar, depending on desired sweetness

2 pints cider vinegar

3 tablespoons salt

2 teaspoons ground ginger

3 teaspoons black pepper

3 teaspoons allspice

½ teaspoon cayenne pepper

The recipe for this condiment came from Simon's grandfather's cook in London. The chutney was a staple in Simon's house in Ireland, and his mother loved making it as much as her family loved eating it. Today, making large batches of chutney is an annual family event in our household in Vermont. The more hands the better! Because of the long, uncovered cooking time and spicy nature of this chutney, make sure there is adequate ventilation in your kitchen. To remove the skins from tomatoes quickly and easily, blanch the tomatoes in boiling water for 15 to 60 seconds, depending on the ripeness and quantity of tomatoes. Using a slotted spoon, briefly dip the tomatoes in ice water, and when they are cool enough to handle, use a small sharp knife to peel off the skins, then core the tomatoes and coarsely chop the flesh. To store the chutney, follow instructions for home canning acid foods and process the chutney in one-pint jars in a boiling-water canner for 20 minutes.

Combine all the ingredients in a 12-quart stockpot.

Bring to a boil over moderate heat and cook, stirring occasionally, for 1 hour.

Reduce the heat to low and simmer, uncovered, for approximately 2 hours, stirring occasionally to prevent the chutney from scorching, until thickened.

Use within a few days served hot, warm, or at room temperature, or for longer storage, can the chutney according to the instructions above.

Ballymaloe Brown Bread

Unsalted butter, for greasing pans

¼ cup unsulphured molasses

1⅓ ounces fresh yeast, or 2 (¼-ounce) packages active dry yeast

3¼ cups warm water

7 cups wholemeal flour

2 teaspoons salt

Simon's mother, Lucy, made a loaf of brown bread in her kitchen in Shanagarry, Ireland, and brought it to the Allen family at Ballymaloe House, a country house hotel nearby. The Allens, stunned by its flavor, began to make it at Ballymaloe's famous restaurant and have served it there ever since. When we brought the recipe to our restaurant in Vermont, we gave it the Ballymaloe name. The distinctive taste of the brown bread at our own restaurant comes from the flour we use, How-ards wholemeal flour, which comes to us from Ireland. Because this flour is not readily available to the home cook, I suggest using a high-quality alternative such as King Arthur's Irish-style wholemeal flour, which is available online and by mail order.

Preheat the oven to 450°F. Grease two 9 by 5 by 3-inch loaf pans.

In a small mixing bowl, combine the molasses and yeast. Add the water and gently whisk to dissolve the yeast and break up any lumps. Let sit for about 10 minutes to activate the yeast.

In a large bowl, whisk together the flour and salt and make a well in the center of the mixture. Pour the yeast mixture into the well and mix gently by hand until thoroughly combined.

Divide the batter evenly between the two prepared loaf pans and allow the batter to rise for 10 to 20 minutes, or until the dough comes to the top of the pans (be careful not to let the loaves over-proof, or the dough will collapse).

Bake the loaves for 20 minutes. Rotate the loaves, turn the heat down to 350°F, and bake for another 20 minutes.

Remove the loaves from the pans, return them to the oven upside-down, placing them directly on an oven rack, and bake for 25 minutes more. When done, the outside of the loaves should be firm.

Rory's Irish Scones

Makes 54 small scones

4 cups all-purpose flour,
plus more for rolling and baking

½ heaping teaspoon baking soda

1 teaspoon salt

½ heaping teaspoon sugar

2 cups buttermilk

Our friend Darina Allen owns and operates the esteemed Ballymaloe Cookery School in Shanagarry, Ireland. This recipe is by Darina's brother, chef Rory O'Connell. Making these scones may seem challenging, but in reality, they are quick and easy to prepare and bake. At our restaurant, we use King Arthur's unbleached bread flour. The dough should be light, fluffy, and springy to the touch, like a marshmallow. The squares of dough should be placed on a baking sheet with space between them; as the dough bakes, the scones will spread and join together. Remove them from the pan in sections and gently separate them; the sides of the scones will remain soft.

Preheat the oven to 400°F.

Sift the flour, baking soda, salt, and sugar into a large mixing bowl. Make a well in the center of the dry mixture and pour in the buttermilk. Mix together by hand just until thoroughly combined (be careful not to overwork the dough, as this causes toughness).

Turn out the dough onto a well-floured surface and form into a large rectangle about 1 inch thick. Using a rolling pin and extra flour as needed, roll out the rectangle until ¾ inch thick.

Using a sharp knife, cut the dough into nine strips about 1 inch wide, then cut each of the strips into six 1-inch squares.

Lightly flour a large baking sheet and arrange the dough squares in nine rows of six, just barely touching.

Bake for 10 minutes, rotate the pan, and bake for another 10 minutes, until the scones are firm but not dry. (If you use a convection oven, bake for 10 minutes, rotate the pan, and bake for 7 minutes more.)

Vermont Cheddar Soup

½ cup grated carrots

½ cup minced celery

½ cup (1 stick) unsalted butter

1 small onion, finely diced

1 teaspoon fresh thyme

1 bay leaf

½ cup all-purpose flour

4 cups hot chicken stock

3 cups grated extra-sharp Vermont Cheddar cheese

1 cup half-and-half

salt and freshly ground black pepper

chopped fresh parsley, for garnish

Be sure to use a Vermont-made, extra-sharp Cheddar cheese. To allow the flavors to fully develop, this soup is best refrigerated and then reheated and served the day after it is made. It should have a creamy, velvety texture with a slight acidic bite and should taste like Cheddar cheese, not chicken stock or thyme (these flavors should remain in the background).

Blanch the carrots and celery in a pot of boiling water. Drain well and set aside.

In a 3-quart soup pot, melt the butter over low heat. Add the onion, thyme, and bay leaf and sauté over medium-high heat until the onions are translucent, about 8 minutes.

Reduce the temperature to a very low heat, whisk in the flour to make a roux (a mixture of melted butter and flour), and cook for about 2 minutes. Turn the heat up to high and continue to cook until the roux is foaming.

Pour the hot stock into the roux, 1 cup at a time, making sure to keep the liquid at a boil, and whisk rapidly until the soup base is smooth.

Add the Cheddar cheese to the soup base in two batches, stirring to combine. Once the cheese has melted, stir in the half-and-half and reserved carrots and celery. Add salt and pepper to taste.

To serve, evenly divide the soup among cups or bowls. Garnish each serving with parsley.

Serves 6 to 8 as a first course
or 4 as a main course

Parsnip and Pear Soup

2 pounds parsnips, peeled
and chopped

3 ripe pears, peeled and chopped

1 sweet onion, peeled and chopped

3 tablespoons unsalted butter

½ cup apple cider vinegar

4 cups apple cider

½ cup heavy cream

1 teaspoon salt

½ teaspoon white pepper

fresh pomegranate seeds or
pomegranate molasses, for garnish

In a 5-quart soup pot over medium heat, sauté the parsnips, pears, and onions in the butter until the onions are translucent. Pour in the cider vinegar and cook until almost dry. Pour in the apple cider and add enough water to just cover the parsnips. Simmer uncovered over low heat for 1 hour, until the parsnips and pears are very tender.

Add the cream. With an immersion blender, purée until smooth, or as an alternate method, transfer the soup base to a blender, add the cream, and purée until smooth. Season the soup with the salt and white pepper.

To serve, evenly divide the soup among cups or bowls. Garnish with pomegranate seeds or a drizzle of pomegranate molasses.

Connemara Broth

8 ounces bacon, diced

1 medium onion, diced

2 cloves garlic, minced

2 large potatoes, peeled and diced

4 to 5 cups chicken stock

⅓ cup tomato paste

4 cups coarsely chopped green cabbage

1 (14½-ounce) can diced tomatoes

1½ teaspoons sugar

1 teaspoon salt

freshly ground black pepper

chopped fresh parsley, for garnish

This traditional Irish broth is truly a hearty soup, perfect for serving on a cold winter day. The fact that it's a one-pot broth is just part of its appeal. If this soup is made in the winter, canned tomatoes are easier to obtain than fresh, and their flesh is more consistent in texture than out-of-season whole tomatoes.

In a 4-quart soup pot, cook the bacon over low heat until brown and crispy, 10 to 15 minutes. Drain off most of the bacon drippings, retaining 1 tablespoon in the pot.

Add the onions and garlic to the bacon and cook over medium-low heat until the onions are tender, about 5 minutes.

Add the potatoes, chicken stock, and tomato paste to the pot and bring to a boil. Reduce the heat and simmer, covered, for 8 minutes.

Stir in the cabbage, tomatoes, sugar, salt, and pepper to taste. Simmer until the potatoes and cabbage are tender, 15 to 20 minutes.

To serve, evenly divide the soup among cups or bowls. Garnish each serving with parsley.

Tomato and White Bean Soup

Serves 6 as a first course
or 4 as a main course

1 large onion, chopped

4 cloves garlic, chopped

¼ cup olive oil

1 tablespoon chopped fresh thyme

1 tablespoon chopped fresh sage

1 cup cooked cannellini beans,
rinsed and drained

½ cup white wine

1 medium roma tomato, cut into
large dice (1 cup)

1½ cups chicken or vegetable stock

2 teaspoons salt

1 teaspoon black pepper

¼ teaspoon crushed red pepper

4 ounces fresh spinach, washed and
coarsely chopped

freshly grated Pecorino Romano
cheese, for serving

In a 3-quart soup pot, sweat the onions and garlic in the olive oil with the thyme and sage.

Add the cannellini beans to the pot, reduce the heat to low, and cook for 10 minutes. Add the wine, tomatoes, and stock and bring to a simmer. Continue to gently simmer for 30 minutes, then season the soup with the salt, black pepper, and red pepper flakes.

Just before serving, stir in the spinach, allowing it to wilt in the hot soup, then evenly divide the soup among cups or bowls. Top with the pecorino and serve.

Mushroom and Leek Soup

Serves 6 as a first course
or 4 as a main course

4 tablespoons unsalted butter

3 tablespoons all-purpose flour

4 cups chicken stock

2 leeks, washed, trimmed, and sliced into ⅛-inch-thick half-moons

1 tablespoon chopped garlic

1 tablespoon chopped fresh thyme

1 pound mixed mushroom caps, sliced

salt and freshly ground white pepper

½ cup heavy cream

green onions or Crispy Leeks, for garnish (recipe below)

Crispy Leeks (optional)

all-purpose flour, for coating

1 to 2 large leeks, cut into matchsticks, gently washed, and thoroughly dried

vegetable oil, for frying

salt

You may use locally foraged mushrooms if you can get your hands on them, but widely available mushrooms such as crimini, oyster, or shiitake (or a mix of all three) will work perfectly, too. To cut a leek into matchsticks, trim off the root end and leaves. Slice the yellow-white stalk in half crosswise, then cut both pieces in half lengthwise to create four pieces. Place them round sides up on the cutting board and carefully slice them into long, thin slices, or matchsticks, about ⅛ inch thick.

Melt 2 tablespoons of the butter in a saucepan over low heat. Whisk in the flour and cook slowly, stirring constantly, until the aroma is lightly nutty and toasted (this is called a blonde roux), about 20 minutes. Slowly whisk in the chicken stock and bring the white sauce (known as a velouté) to a simmer.

Meanwhile, in another saucepan over medium heat, sweat the leeks, garlic, and thyme in the remaining 2 tablespoons butter until the leeks are soft, about 10 minutes. Add the mushrooms and the sauce and continue to cook for about 5 minutes, until the flavors meld. Season with salt and white pepper to taste (depending on the flavor of the chicken broth used in the velouté). Whisk in the heavy cream and evenly divide the soup among cups or bowls. Garnish with thinly sliced green onions or the crispy leeks and serve.

Crispy Leeks

Place some flour in a bowl, add the leeks, and toss the matchsticks to coat. Shake off excess flour and place the coated leek sticks in a single layer on a baking sheet.

Heat ¼ inch of the oil in a 10-inch frying pan and fry the leeks, in batches as necessary, until golden brown and crispy. Remove to paper towels to drain. Salt to taste.

A few years ago, we renovated part of the Mill in Quechee and added a bar, wanting to create an informal setting where visitors to the store could relax and enjoy some light food, and for restaurant guests to enjoy a drink before dinner. The bar is also a popular gathering place for our family and friends.

Above left, Andrew, and above right, Kevin, greet a friend.

Right: Me with our friend, Ann Suokko, in the foreground.

Opposite: The bar offers a beer flight featuring four beers from Vermont breweries presented in our Ludlow Whiskey Glass Set (see pages 138-9 for a sample flight menu).

On the following series of pages are Simon, Andrew, Adam, Kevin, and me with friends Ann and Gertrude Suokko, and Jerod Rockwell behind the bar.

Blue Moon Sparkler

Sparkling wine
1 small scoop Blue Moon Sorbet
(visit bluemoonsorbet.com for info
on where to buy)

Pour your favorite sparkling wine
into a Simon Pearce Hartland flute
glass, leaving room for the sorbet.
Float the scoop of sorbet on top.

Pomegranate Margarita

Combine in a cocktail shaker
and shake well:
2 ounces El Charro Silver Tequila
1 ounce Cointreau
2 ounces sour mix
1 ounce POM/Pama mix (equal
parts pomegranate juice and Pama
Pomegranate Liqueur)

Pour into a salt-rimmed Simon
Pearce Ascutney rocks glass.
Garnish with a lime wedge.

Maple Bourbon Manhattan

Fill a Simon Pearce Ascutney
whiskey glass with ice. Pour the
following ingredients over the
ice and mix:
1¾ ounces No. 14 Maple Bourbon
½ ounces Sapling Maple Liqueur
Dash maple bitters

Garnish with a Luxardo
maraschino cherry.

Beer

"Extra Stout" ~ Burlington · VT
Zero Gravity Brewing 5.9%

"Green State Lager" ~ Burlington · VT
Zero Gravity Brewing 4.9%

"Society & Solitude" ~ Greensboro · VT
Hill Farmstead - NEIPA 8.1%

"Chinooker'D" ~ Waitsfield · VT
Lawsons Finest Liquids IPA 6.5%

"Super Session #2" ~ Waitsfield · VT
Lawsons Finest Liquids IPA 4.8%

"Rainbow Red Ale" ~ Springfield · VT
Trout River Brewing 4.8%

~ TRY A FLIGHT ~

Arugula and Brussels Sprout Salad

1 pound Brussels sprouts

olive oil, for coating the sprouts

salt and freshly ground black pepper

12 ounces baby arugula

½ cup dried cranberries

½ cup hazelnuts, toasted and chopped

Warm Bacon Vinaigrette to taste
(recipe below)

¼ cup freshly grated Pecorino
Romano cheese, for serving

Warm Bacon Vinaigrette

Makes 2 cups

8 ounces roughly chopped bacon

1 shallot, minced

1 clove garlic, minced

½ cup red wine vinegar

4 tablespoons maple syrup

½ cup olive oil

1 teaspoon chopped fresh thyme

½ teaspoon black pepper

Preheat the oven to 350°F.

Remove and discard the core from the base of each Brussels sprout. Separate or thinly slice the leaves and toss them with olive oil and salt and pepper to taste.

Spread the sprout leaves in a single layer on a baking sheet and bake for 5 to 7 minutes, until the leaves crisp up.

Toss the arugula, cranberries, hazelnuts, and warm Brussels sprouts with the vinaigrette. Sprinkle with the pecorino and serve.

Warm Bacon Vinaigrette

In a 12-inch skillet, cook the bacon until the fat is rendered and the bacon is crispy. Add the shallot and garlic and cook until the vegetables are soft. Pour in the vinegar, maple syrup, and olive oil and bring the liquid to a simmer.

Carefully transfer the contents of the skillet to a blender and purée until smooth. Add the thyme and pepper and pulse to combine.

The vinaigrette should be served warm, so be sure to reheat it if not serving immediately.

Serves 4

Field Greens Salad

1 (4-ounce) log goat cheese

½ cup panko bread crumbs

2 tablespoons melted butter

1 teaspoon fresh or dried thyme

1 teaspoon fresh or dried parsley

½ teaspoon minced garlic (optional)

1 pound mixed field greens

Simon Pearce Vinaigrette to taste (recipe below)

6 or 8 vine-ripe cherry tomatoes, cut in half

12 cucumber slices or endive spears

Simon Pearce Vinaigrette

Makes 2 cups

¼ cup fresh lemon juice

¼ cup malt vinegar

1 clove garlic, chopped

1 teaspoon dried basil

1 teaspoon salt

½ teaspoon freshly ground black pepper

1½ cups olive oil

¼ cup chopped fresh parsley

We suggest using Vermont Butter & Cheese Company goat cheese, or the highest-quality local goat cheese you can find. At the Simon Pearce restaurant, our chefs use panko Japanese bread crumbs for coating the cheese because the panko crumbs are lighter than most available bread crumbs. Be sure to make the Simon Pearce House Vinaigrette ahead of time to allow the flavors to meld.

Preheat the broiler.

Cut the goat cheese crosswise into four even slices. In a small bowl, mix together the bread crumbs, melted butter, thyme, parsley, and garlic (if using). Place the goat cheese slices directly in the bowl of bread crumbs and gently toss and pat them to coat with the mixture.

Gently place the coated cheese slices on a small baking sheet, brown under the broiler, and set aside.

In a mixing bowl, toss the field greens with vinaigrette to taste. Divide the salad greens among chilled plates. Place the tomato halves around the greens and the cucumber slices on top. Finish with the slices of warm goat cheese and serve.

Simon Pearce Vinaigrette

Combine the lemon juice, vinegar, garlic, basil, salt, and pepper in a blender and pulse to combine. While the blender is running, slowly stream in the olive oil until emulsified. Add the parsley and pulse for 10 seconds, or until the vinaigrette is creamy, smooth, and green in color.

Charred Broccolini and Shishito Peppers

2 bunches broccolini, trimmed and blanched

olive oil, for sautéing

2 cloves garlic, chopped

1 shallot, thinly grated

1 tablespoon white wine

2 tablespoons unsalted butter

¼ cup golden raisins

2 tablespoons pumpkin seeds, toasted

Charred Shishito Peppers (recipe below)

salt and freshly ground black pepper

½ cup Vadouvan Curry Aioli (recipe below)

Shishito Peppers

2 tablespoons olive oil

1 pound shishito peppers (or substitute poblano peppers)

2 teaspoons coarse salt

Vadouvan Curry Aioli

Makes 1 cup

1 cup mayonnaise

2 tablespoons vadouvan curry powder (contains French aromatics like grated shallots and garlic), or curry powder of your choosing

Juice and zest of 1 lime

salt

In a sauté pan over medium-high heat, sauté the broccolini in olive oil until the tips of the broccolini begin to brown, 5 to 7 minutes. Add the garlic and shallot and cook until the vegetables start to caramelize.

Deglaze the pan with the wine, add the butter, and continue to cook the broccolini until tender and caramelized. Add the raisins, pumpkin seeds, and shishito peppers, toss together, and cook until the wine and butter are completely absorbed or evaporated. Season to taste with salt and pepper.

To serve, spread aioli on each plate, then divide the broccolini and shishito mixture evenly on top of the aioli.

Shishito Peppers

Heat the olive oil in a sauté pan over medium-high heat. Carefully add the peppers to the hot oil and allow them to blister on all sides, seasoning with the salt as you turn them. Remove from the pan once the peppers have blistered all over and begun to soften.

Vadouvan Curry Aioli

Combine the mayonnaise, curry powder, and lime juice and zest in a small bowl and stir until the curry powder has dissolved completely. Adjust the seasoning with salt.

Seared Tuna Crudo

Serves 4 to 6

1 pound trimmed sushi-grade tuna, cut into 2 x 2 x 4-inch blocks (ask your fishmonger for number-one-grade fatty tuna, if available)

2 tablespoons chopped fresh parsley

1 tablespoon black pepper

1 teaspoon salt

2 tablespoons olive oil, plus more for coating the vegetables

¼ cup finely diced celery root (⅛-inch cubes are ideal for all the root vegetables)

¼ cup finely diced carrots

¼ cup finely diced parsnips

olive oil, to coat

salt

Wasabi Aioli (recipe below)

fresh cilantro leaves, for garnish

pickled ginger, for garnish

Wasabi Aioli

Makes a generous ½ cup

½ cup mayonnaise

1 tablespoon wasabi paste

1 tablespoon mirin

1 teaspoon rice wine vinegar

1 tablespoon liquid from jar of pickled ginger

Roll the blocks of tuna in the parsley and black pepper and season with the salt.

Heat the olive oil in a skillet over medium-high heat. Evenly sear the tuna on all sides and quickly remove to a plate (do not overcook it—the center of sushi-grade tuna should remain raw).

Chill the seared tuna in the refrigerator to firm up the fish. Once firm, use a sharp chef's knife to slice the tuna into ¼-inch-thick slabs.

Quickly blanch the celery, carrot, and parsnip cubes in salted water, rapidly chill them in ice water, drain, and allow them to dry. Once dry, toss the vegetables in olive oil and salt to taste.

To serve, using a large serving spoon or plastic spatula, spread aioli across a plate in a long push. Shingle the tuna slices on one side of the aioli. Spoon a line of the tiny cubes of vegetables along one side of the tuna slices. Repeat to create four servings. Garnish with the cilantro and pickled ginger.

Wasabi Aioli

In a bowl, stir together the mayonnaise, wasabi paste, mirin, vinegar, and liquid from pickled ginger. Refrigerate until ready to use.

Smoked Salmon Canapés

1 loaf Ballymaloe Brown Bread (recipe on page 108) or pumpernickel, sliced and toasted

8 ounces thinly sliced smoked salmon, separated and rolled

Horseradish Aioli (recipe below), in squeeze bottle or plastic bag with corner cut off

Your Choice of Garnishes

Pickled Red Onions (recipe below)

capers, rinsed and drained

fresh dill sprigs

zest of 1 lemon

Horseradish Aioli

Makes 1 cup

¾ cup mayonnaise

¼ cup crème fraîche

1 tablespoons prepared horseradish

3 drops Worcestershire sauce

1 teaspoon black pepper

Pickled Red Onions

Makes 1 cup

½ cup red wine vinegar

juice of 2 limes

1 red onion, cut into matchsticks, gently washed, and thoroughly dried

Cut the crusts off the toast and cut each slice into 2 by 2-inch squares to make 32 bite-size pieces in all.

Roll up each slice of smoked salmon, then cut each roll crosswise into 2-inch pieces.

To assemble, squeeze a generous dollop of the aioli onto each square of toast. Top each with a small roll of smoked salmon. Garnish with your choice of pickled red onions, capers, dill sprigs, and lemon zest (whatever combination you like best).

Horseradish Aioli

In a small bowl, whisk together the mayonnaise, crème fraiche, horseradish, Worcestershire sauce, and pepper. Refrigerate until ready to use, then transfer to a squeeze bottle or a zip-tight bag with one corner cut off.

Pickled Red Onions

In a small saucepan, combine the vinegar, ½ cup water, and the lime juice and bring to boil. Pour the brine over the red onions and chill them in the refrigerator until ready to use. Leftovers may be stored in an airtight container in the refrigerator for up to 4 weeks.

Tenderloin of Beef Crostini

1 pound beef tenderloin (the tip end of the tenderloin works well for this)

2 tablespoon chopped fresh flat-leaf parsley, plus additional sprigs, for garnish

1 tablespoon black pepper

1 teaspoon salt

2 tablespoons olive oil, for cooking

32 baguette slices, toasted

Dijonaise (recipe below)

Caper Onion Relish (recipe below)

Dijonaise

Makes a generous ½ cup

½ cup mayonnaise

2 tablespoons Dijon mustard

1 teaspoon fresh lemon juice

Caper Onion Relish

Makes 1 cup

1 small red onion, minced

3 tablespoons chopped capers

2 tablespoons chopped fresh parsley

½ teaspoon olive oil

Preheat the oven to 325°F.

Roll the tenderloin in the chopped parsley, black pepper, and salt. Heat the olive oil in a roasting pan over medium-high heat, add the tenderloin to the pan, and sear all sides evenly.

Roast in the oven until the internal temperature of the beef reaches 130°F, about 12 minutes.

Chill the beef in the refrigerator for 15 minutes or more to firm it up (warm beef can be difficult to slice uniformly), then slice the tenderloin into thick pieces about the same dimensions as the crostini you will be serving them on.

To assemble, spread ¾ teaspoon of dijonaise on each crostini. Top each crostini with a slice of beef, a teaspoon of the caper onion relish, and a sprig of parsley. Arrange on a serving platter.

Dijonaise

In a small bowl, stir together the mayonnaise, mustard, and lemon juice. Refrigerate until ready to use.

Caper Onion Relish

In a small bowl, stir together the onion, capers, parsley, and olive oil.

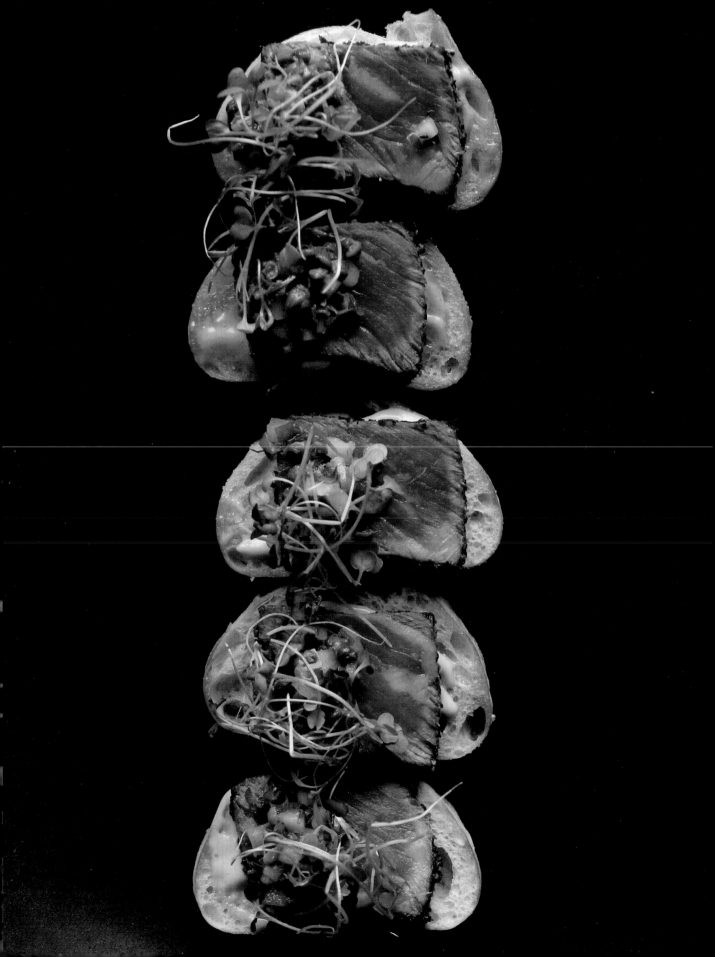

Simon Pearce Restaurant director, Jerod Rockwell, in the Pearce's home kitchen searing shrimp for our Thai Red Curry Shrimp recipe on pages 154–55.

Thai Red Curry Shrimp

3 tablespoons olive oil

16–20 shrimp, peeled and deveined, tails removed

Thai Curry Sauce (recipe below)

½ cup jicama, cut into matchsticks

½ cup small-diced pineapple

2 tablespoons fresh cilantro leaves

¼ cup raw peanuts, toasted

Jasmine Rice with Lime and Coconut (recipe below)

Thai Curry Sauce

Makes 2 cups

2 tablespoons olive oil

1 leek, washed, root end and greens trimmed, and white part thinly sliced

1-inch length of fresh ginger, sliced

3 tablespoons store-bought red curry paste

2 tablespoons brown sugar

12 ounces canned coconut milk

Jasmine Rice with Lime and Coconut

Makes 2 cups

1 cup long-grain jasmine rice

1 tablespoon unsalted butter

1 teaspoon salt

2 kaffir lime leaves (or 1 teaspoon lime zest)

1 teaspoon lime zest

2 tablespoons unsweetened coconut flakes

Heat 2 tablespoons of the oil in a large saucepan over medium heat. Working in batches if necessary, add the shrimp in a single layer and sear them, turning once.

Pour in the curry sauce and bring the liquid to a simmer, letting the shrimp absorb the flavors and finish cooking (the shrimp should not be opaque). Keep warm.

Just before serving, toss together the jicama and pineapple with the cilantro leaves, peanuts, and remaining 1 tablespoon olive oil.

To serve, divide the rice among four bowls. Place 4 or 5 shrimp on top of each serving and divide the remaining curry sauce over the shrimp. Garnish each serving with the jicama-pineapple mixture.

Thai Curry Sauce

Heat the oil in a heavy-bottomed saucepan over medium heat. Add the leek and ginger and cook until the vegetables begin to caramelize, about 6 minutes.

Reduce the heat to low, stir in the curry paste, and cook for 3 minutes. Add the brown sugar and stir until dissolved. Pour in the coconut milk and simmer over medium heat for 15 minutes until the sauce thickens. Remove from the heat.

Jasmine Rice with Lime and Coconut

Rinse the rice until the water runs clear. Place in a saucepan with 2 cups water, the butter, salt, and lime leaf. Bring to boil, cover, and reduce the heat to a simmer. Continue to simmer for about 20 minutes, or until the rice is tender and the water is absorbed. Remove from the heat and stir in the lime zest and coconut.

Roasted Heirloom Carrots

16 peeled heirloom baby carrots

2 tablespoons olive oil

¼ cup raw cashews

2 teaspoons ground sumac

1 teaspoon salt

1 teaspoon black pepper

½ cup orange juice

Sumac Yogurt (recipe below)

Curried Cashew Brittle (recipe below)

toasted pumpkin seeds, for garnish

fresh herbs, such as flat-leaf parsley sprigs, for garnish

Curried Cashew Brittle

Makes 12 ounces

2 teaspoons butter

1 cup sugar

½ cup corn syrup

1 teaspoon baking soda

1 teaspoon curry powder

1½ cups raw cashews

Sumac Yogurt

Makes 1 cup

2 teaspoons ground sumac

1 tablespoon fresh lime juice

1 cup plain Greek yogurt

1 tablespoon honey

1 teaspoon salt

Preheat the oven to 350°F.

In a shallow baking dish, toss together the carrots, oil, cashews, sumac, salt, pepper, and orange juice. Cover with aluminum foil and bake the carrots for 25 minutes. Uncover and cook for another 15 minutes, or until the carrots are slightly tender.

To serve, spread a scoop of yogurt on a plate and top with one-fourth of the carrots. Sprinkle some curried cashew brittle and toasted pumpkin seeds over the top. Repeat to create 4 servings total. Garnish each one with flat-leaf parsley or other fresh herbs.

Curried Cashew Brittle

Grease a baking sheet with 1 teaspoon of the butter and set aside.

Combine the sugar and corn syrup in a microwave-safe bowl and microwave uncovered for 3 minutes. Stir to dissolve the sugar and microwave for another 2 minutes.

Stir in the remaining teaspoon of butter and the cashews and microwave for an additional 40 seconds. Continue to microwave at 20-second intervals until a light amber color is achieved.

Remove the bowl from the microwave and very carefully stir in the baking soda and curry powder. Spread the caramel mixture in a thin layer on the prepared baking sheet and allow to cool completely, about 20 minutes.

When the brittle is hard, break it into small pieces.

Sumac Yogurt

Stir together the sumac and lime juice until the sumac dissolves.

In a small bowl, combine the yogurt, honey, and salt. Pour the lime juice mixture into the yogurt and stir until well combined. Refrigerate until ready to serve.

Cauliflower Gratin

Serves 4

2 large heads cauliflower

½ cup (1 stick) unsalted butter

3 cloves garlic, chopped

2 shallots, sliced

2 pounds cauliflower florets (use the trim from the steaks, plus additional to equal 2 pounds)

½ cup heavy cream

salt and freshly ground black pepper

olive oil, for greasing the baking dish

1 cup grated aged Cheddar cheese

Lentil Salad (recipe follows)

micro greens, for garnish (optional)

Lentil Salad

Makes 3 cups

½ cup salted pepitas (pumpkin seeds)

½ cup white balsamic vinegar

Canola or corn oil, for frying

¼ cup fresh sage leaves

¾ cup dried Red Chief lentils (or other variety of lentils)

1 cinnamon stick

¾ cup roasted red peppers, cut into matchsticks

½ cup golden raisins

¼ cup olive oil

Preheat the oven to 325°F.

Cut four 1-inch "steaks" from the center of each head of cauliflower for a total of eight steaks. Save the trimmed ends for the purée.

Melt the butter in a large saucepan over medium heat. Continue to cook the butter until it begins to brown and release a nutty aroma. Add the garlic and shallots and cook until they start to caramelize. Reduce the heat to low, add the cauliflower florets and cook them, stirring frequently, until the cauliflower releases its water content and starts to fall apart. Pour in the cream and bring to simmer. Transfer to a blender and purée until smooth and velvety. Season with salt and pepper and set aside.

Coat a roasting pan with olive oil, lay the cauliflower steaks out flat, and season with salt and pepper. Cover the pan with aluminum foil and bake for 15–20 minutes, or until a toothpick can be easily inserted through the cauliflower.

Remove the foil and sprinkle the cheese over the steaks. Return to the oven and broil until the cheese is browned.

To serve, smear the cauliflower purée on a plate, top with the cauliflower steaks, and serve the lentil salad alongside. Garnish with microgreens, if desired.

Lentil Salad

Toast the pumpkin seeds in a nonstick skillet until they are just a little crispy.

In a small saucepan over low heat, bring the balsamic vinegar to a boil and reduce it by half until it is thick and syrupy. Remove from the heat.

Heat ¼ inch oil in a saucepan over medium heat and fry the sage leaves until crispy and aromatic. Transfer to paper towels to drain.

Put the lentils and cinnamon stick in another small saucepan and add heavily salted water to cover. Bring to a boil, then turn down the heat and simmer for 20–25 minutes until al dente. Drain and let cool.

In a medium bowl, gently toss together the lentils, red peppers, raisins, pumpkin seeds, vinegar reduction, and olive oil. Crumble the fried sage leaves into the salad and toss again. Serve at room temperature. Can be prepared one day in advance and refrigerated until serving time.

Quinoa-Stuffed Peppers

Serves 4

4 red bell peppers

olive oil, for coating

salt and freshly ground black pepper

Quinoa Stuffing (recipe follows)

crumbled chèvre, for topping

1 cup Roasted Pepper Marinara
(recipe below), for drizzling

Quinoa Stuffing

Makes 4 cups

1 small onion, cut into small dice

2 cloves garlic, chopped

½ cup small-diced zucchini

½ cup small-diced bell pepper (use
the tops of the peppers to be stuffed)

olive oil, for cooking

1 cup black quinoa

1 tablespoon adobo from canned
chipotles in adobo (optional,
depending on desired heat)

½ cup Roasted Pepper Marinara
(recipe below)

1 cup roughly chopped fresh spinach

¼ cup crumbled chèvre (optional)

Roasted Pepper Marinara

Makes 6 cups

1 small sweet onion, diced

3 cloves garlic, crushed

¼ teaspoon crushed red pepper

3 tablespoons olive oil

1 (24-ounce) can San Marzano whole
peeled tomatoes

¼ cup roasted red bell peppers

Preheat the oven to 350°F.

Slice the tops off the bell peppers and trim the bottoms so that they will sit level (save the tops for the quinoa stuffing, below).

Toss the peppers in olive oil to coat and season with salt and pepper. Roast them in a baking dish for 7 or 8 minutes (they should just start to soften).

Divide the stuffing evenly among the peppers (about 1 cup per pepper) and sprinkle the tops with chèvre. Return the peppers to the oven and bake for another 10 minutes.

To serve, spoon some marinara on each plate and place one pepper on top.

Quinoa Stuffing

In a saucepan over medium heat, sweat the onion, garlic, zucchini, and bell pepper in some olive oil. Add the quinoa and let it toast slightly.

Pour in 2 cups water, the adobo, and the marinara and bring to a simmer. Stir in the spinach, cover, and let cook for about 15 minutes, or until the liquid is absorbed. Fold the chèvre into the stuffing, if desired. Can be made one day ahead. Bring to room temperature before stuffing the peppers.

Roasted Pepper Marinara

In a saucepan over medium heat, sweat the onion, garlic, and red pepper flakes in the olive oil.

Add the tomatoes and roasted red peppers and simmer on a very low heat for about an hour.

Purée in a standing blender (or use a hand blender) until smooth.

Roasted Vegetable Pappardelle

Pesto

Makes 1 cup

½ cup pine nuts

2 cups loosely packed fresh basil leaves

1 tablespoon coarse salt

½ cup olive oil

1 cup grated Grana Padano or hard cheese of your choice

Roasted Mushrooms and Vegetables

3 ounces crimini, hen of the woods, or maitake mushroom, depending on season and availability

extra-virgin olive oil

salt and freshly ground black pepper

3–4 sprigs fresh thyme

¼ medium zucchini, cut into ½-inch half-moons (about ½ cup)

3 to 4 cherry tomatoes, left whole

Assemble the Pasta

1 pound pappardelle (De Cecco makes a quality version)

¼ cup olive oil

2 cloves garlic, thinly grated

1 shallot, thinly grated

¼ cup white wine

2 tablespoons unsalted butter

1 cup loosely packed baby spinach

½ cup grated Grana Padano or hard cheese of your choice, for serving

Pesto

In a food processor, pulse the pine nuts until they form a paste. Add the basil and the salt and pulse until the basil is incorporated into the pine nut paste. Add the oil and cheese and pulse a few times to incorporate. (See Alternate Method)

Alternate method: In a mortar and pestle, grind the pine nuts until they form a soft paste. Add the basil and salt and grind until the basil is incorporated into the pine nut paste (you may need to add a little basil at a time, depending on the size of your mortar and pestle). Drizzle the olive oil into the mixture, add the cheese, and grind until the pesto is thoroughly mixed.

Roasted Mushrooms and Vegetables

Preheat the oven to 375°F.

Cut the mushrooms into wedges and arrange them in a single layer on a baking sheet. Drizzle with oil and season with salt and pepper. Lay the thyme sprigs on top and roast until tender, about 12 minutes.

Toss the zucchini and the cherry tomatoes in a little bit of pesto, arrange them in a single layer on another baking sheet, and roast until al dente, about 10 minutes.

Assemble the Pasta

Cook the pasta according to package directions, drain, and set aside.

Heat the olive oil in a 9-inch sauté pan over medium heat, add the garlic and shallot, and sweat them. Add the pre-roasted mushrooms and vegetables and cook until they start to caramelize.

Pour in the wine and let simmer until the pan is almost dry. Reduce the heat to low, add the butter and pesto along with the spinach and cooked pasta, and toss to coat. Leave on low heat, tossing frequently, until the pasta has been warmed through and the spinach has wilted.

To serve, divide the pasta and vegetables among bowls and top with the grana padano.

Simon Pearce Restaurant executive chef, Jeremy Conway, in the Pearce's home kitchen arranging fillets during a recipe tasting for our Herb-Seared Atlantic Halibut recipe on the following pages.

Herb-Seared Atlantic Halibut

Serves 4

Spiced Corn Sauce

Makes 2 cups

6 ears corn, husks and silks removed

1 poblano pepper

1 cup heavy cream

2 teaspoons sherry wine vinegar

juice of 1 lime

Corn Relish

6 ears corn, husks and silks removed

2 poblano peppers

1 small red onion

¼ cup loosely packed fresh cilantro leaves

1 tablespoon sherry wine vinegar

2 tablespoons olive oil

juice and zest of 1 lime

1 teaspoon salt

½ teaspoon black pepper

Preparation

4 (6-ounce) Atlantic halibut fillets, skin removed

salt and freshly ground black pepper

4 tablespoons olive oil

4 tablespoons unsalted butter

3 cloves garlic, grated

2 shallots, grated

2 ounces fingerling potatoes, blanched and cut into discs

½ cup fresh corn kernels

1 pint cherry tomatoes, halved

¼ cup loosely packed fresh cilantro leaves

1 bunch baby spinach, sautéed

Spiced Corn Sauce

Cut the corn from the cob and purée the kernels in a blender. Pour the purée into a saucepan and cook over very low heat until the corn begins to thicken slightly.

Meanwhile, char the poblano pepper with a kitchen torch (or caramelize under the broiler on high heat for 10 minutes or until charred), trim off the top, remove the seeds, and peel away the blistered skin.

Add the poblano to the corn purée along with the cream, vinegar, and lime juice and cook for another 10 minutes, until the pepper is soft. Transfer the sauce to the blender and purée until smooth.

Corn Relish

Roast the corn in the oven at 350°F for 12 minutes. Let cool then cut the kernels from the cob.

Char and clean the poblanos as described for the corn sauce (above) and cut the peppers into ¼-inch dice. Finely chop the red onion.

In a bowl, combine the roasted corn, poblanos, and red onion. Add the cilantro, vinegar, oil, lime zest and juice, salt, and pepper and toss to mix. Can be made ahead and refrigerated up to 3 days.

Preparation

Preheat the oven to 350°F.

Season the halibut on all sides with salt and pepper. In a large skillet over medium-high heat, sear the fish in the olive oil and 2 tablespoons of the butter. Keeping the seared side of the halibut down, transfer the skillet to the preheated oven and roast for an additional 12 minutes, or until the internal temperature of the fish reaches 150°F.

Meanwhile, heat the remaining 2 tablespoons butter in another skillet over medium-high heat, add the garlic and shallot, and cook for a minute or two. Add the potatoes and corn and cook until a nice crust forms on the potatoes. Add the tomatoes, cilantro leaves, and sautéed spinach, toss to combine, season with salt and pepper, and warm until heated through.

To serve, ladle the spiced corn sauce onto a plate and scoop ½ cup of the corn relish in the center of the sauce. Place a spoonful of the sautéed vegetables over the corn relish. Place a piece of fish on top of the sautéed vegetables and garnish with more relish. Repeat with the other servings.

Serves 8 to 12

Vermont Cheddar Quiche

A deep 9-inch pie plate or baking dish is required for this thick quiche. Your choice of fillings such as ham and spinach, or crab and leek, or any combination of vegetables would work well. Layering the cheese creates a wonderful, crisp top crust.

Crust

½ cup (1 stick) cold unsalted butter, cut into small cubes

1½ cups King Arthur all-purpose white flour, plus more for rolling

1 large egg

⅓ cup ice water

Custard

24 ounces extra-sharp Vermont Cheddar cheese, grated

8 ounces filling of your choice (see Note)

8 large eggs

2 cups heavy cream

¾ teaspoon salt

¼ teaspoon black pepper

Crust

Using a pastry blender or two knives, cut the butter into the flour until the mixture resembles coarse crumbs. Add the egg and ice water and mix until a dough forms. Turn the dough into a ball and place it onto a lightly floured surface and let rest for 20 minutes.

After 20 minutes, roll the dough into a 10-inch circle. Line a deep 9-inch pie plate or baking dish with the dough and crimp the edges. Refrigerate the dough-lined pie plate for at least 1 hour.

Custard

Preheat the oven to 300°F.

Fill the dough-lined pie plate with one-third of the grated cheese. Place filling of your choice on top of the cheese. Top with the remaining two-thirds of grated cheese.

In a bowl, whisk together the eggs and cream until well combined. Season with the salt and pepper. Create a well in the center of the cheese and filling mixture in the baking dish and pour in the egg mixture.

Place the pie plate on a baking sheet and bake for 1 hour. Rotate the baking sheet and pie plate and bake for an additional 45 minutes, or until the quiche is set and the crust is golden brown.

Allow the quiche to rest for 10 minutes before slicing and serving.

Grilled Chicken Sandwiches

4 boneless, skinless chicken breasts

Simon Pearce Vinaigrette (recipe on page 142)

1 French baguette

Parmesan Aioli (recipe below)

½ cup sliced roasted red peppers

4 large lettuce leaves

Parmesan Aioli

Makes a generous ¾ cup

¾ cup mayonnaise

1 tablespoon minced garlic

¾ cup grated Parmesan cheese

1 teaspoon chopped fresh thyme

1 teaspoon chopped fresh parsley

freshly ground black pepper

A fresh, crusty baguette and free-range chicken will provide the best-tasting results. Roasted red peppers marinated in olive oil are readily available at good grocers. The Parmesan aioli and marinated chicken both can be made a day ahead of time.

Marinate the chicken breasts in the vinaigrette for a minimum of 30 minutes at room temperature, or overnight in the refrigerator.

Preheat an outdoor grill or a large ridged grill pan to medium heat. Shake excess marinade off the chicken. Place the chicken breasts on the grill and cook for 10–12 minutes, turning once, until the internal temperature is 165°F and the juices run clear when thickest part of breast is pierced with the tip of a knife. Transfer the chicken breasts to a cutting board and slice them in half horizontally.

Cut the baguette crosswise into four equal pieces and cut each piece in half horizontally. Generously spread each half with Parmesan aioli, covering them completely. Place the bread under a preheated broiler and broil until golden brown.

To assemble the sandwiches, fill the baguettes with sliced roasted red peppers on the bottom, grilled chicken in the middle, and leaf lettuce on top. Serve immediately.

Parmesan Aioli

In a medium bowl, use a spatula to mix together the mayonnaise, garlic, cheese, thyme, parsley, and pepper to taste until well combined. Allow to rest for at least a 30 minutes before serving so the flavors have time to develop.

Serves 4

Mediterranean Lamb Burger

1½ pounds ground lamb

2 tablespoons chopped sun-dried tomatoes

2 tablespoons crumbled feta cheese

2 tablespoons chopped, pitted Kalamata olives

2 tablespoons chopped fresh basil

1 teaspoon dried oregano

2 tablespoons olive oil

salt and black pepper

4 French-style rolls

Rosemary Aioli (recipe below)

4 large lettuce leaves

Rosemary Aioli

½ cup mayonnaise

2 teaspoons finely chopped fresh rosemary

1 clove garlic, minced

salt and freshly ground black pepper

A good, fresh, soft roll makes all the difference when serving this delicious variation on a traditional burger. At our restaurant, we use locally raised lamb from Northeast Family Farms, and accent it with Mediterranean flavors. The rosemary aioli can be made a day in advance so that the flavors have time to develop.

Place the ground lamb in a large mixing bowl, add the sun-dried tomatoes, feta cheese, olives, basil, oregano, and olive oil and, using your hands or a wooden spoon, mix until the ingredients are evenly distributed. Divide the lamb mixture into four patties and season them with salt and pepper to taste.

Preheat an outdoor grill or a large ridged grill pan to medium-high heat. Grill the lamb patties for 3 minutes per side, or to desired doneness.

To serve, cut the rolls in half and spread the bottom halves of each roll with some rosemary aioli. Top with the lamb burgers, lettuce, and top halves of the roll.

Rosemary Aioli

Mix together the mayonnaise, rosemary, and garlic in a small bowl. Add salt and pepper to taste.

Crispy Duck Confit

Serves 4

Duck Legs

2 tablespoon sugar

¼ cup coarse salt

4 duck legs

8 sprigs fresh thyme

1 head garlic

1½ quarts duck fat

Farro

Makes 2 cups

2 cups chicken broth

1 cup farro, rinsed

¼ cup dried black currants

¼ cup chopped dried apricots

salt and freshly ground black pepper

Gastrique

Makes 1 cup

1 cup red wine *ver jus* or red wine vinegar

1 cup red wine

1 (12-ounce) jar huckleberry or blackberry preserves

Duck Legs

Mix together the sugar and coarse salt. On a baking sheet, evenly dust the duck legs with the sugar-salt mixture, lay one thyme sprig over each leg, and wrap the pan tightly with plastic wrap. Refrigerate for 24 hours, then remove the plastic, rinse the legs, and dry them with a paper towel.

Preheat the oven to 225°F.

Over medium heat, sear the skin side of the duck legs until golden brown, then transfer them to a deep baking dish. Cut the garlic head in half across the equator, splitting the cloves, and place the garlic and the remaining 4 sprigs of thyme into a baking dish. Heat the duck fat until it is liquified and pour enough of the fat into the dish to just cover the duck legs.

Roast the duck in the preheated oven for 3–4 hours, or until the leg bone can be easily moved in the joint of a leg. Remove the legs from the fat and drain on paper towels (the duck fat can be strained, stored, and reused.)

Set the oven to broil. Return the duck legs to the baking dish and broil, skin side up, until the skin is crisp.

Farro

Meanwhile, bring the chicken broth to a boil. Add the farro, reduce the heat to a simmer, and cook for 20–25 minutes, or until all the broth has been absorbed and the farro is tender. Stir in the dried currants and apricots and season with salt and pepper.

Gastrique

Just before serving, combine the *ver jus* and red wine in a saucepan and reduce the liquid over medium heat until a syrup consistency is achieved. Stir in half of the preserves and simmer for 5 minutes, until the sauce has thickened slightly.

To serve, place a mound of farro in the center of a plate, top with a duck leg, and drizzle the gastrique around the edge of the farro. Repeat with the other servings. Use the remaining half jar of huckleberry preserves to brush the legs.

Our Roasted Vegetable Pappardelle
recipe on pages 162–63.

Opposite: Pia with Simon Pearce
Restaurant director, Jerod
Rockwell, in the Pearce's home
kitchen preparing our Roasted
Heirloom Carrots recipe on pages
156–57.

Walnut Meringue

Meringue Discs

8 large egg whites

1 teaspoon fresh lemon juice

2¼ cups granulated sugar

2 teaspoons vanilla extract

2 cups walnuts, chopped, plus more for garnish (optional)

Whipped Cream

Makes 2 cups

2 cups heavy cream

2 tablespoons confectioners' sugar

Balsamic Strawberries

Makes 3 cups

¼ cup balsamic vinegar

2 tablespoons light brown sugar

⅛ teaspoon vanilla extract

12 ounces strawberries, hulled and halved

Strawberry Sauce

Makes 2 cups

2 pints strawberries, hulled

2 tablespoons granulated sugar

2 teaspoons fresh lemon juice

Meringue Discs

Preheat the oven to 325°F.

In large bowl, beat the egg whites on low speed until frothy. Add the lemon juice and gradually add the granulated sugar while the mixer is running, then increase the speed to medium-high and beat until the meringue batter holds stiff peaks. Add the vanilla and beat for another 30 seconds to incorporate. Fold in the walnuts with a rubber spatula.

Place the batter in a disposable piping bag with a ½-inch hole cut at the tip. Pipe 2-inch discs spaced 2 inches apart onto a Silpat or non-stick cookie sheet. You'll have 12–16 discs.

Bake in the middle of the oven for 50 to 60 minutes, or until the meringues are puffed up and golden. Transfer the meringues to wire racks to cool completely.

Whipped Cream

In a standing mixer (or by hand with a whisk), whip the cream to soft peaks. Add the confectioners' sugar and continue to whip for another 30 seconds to incorporate it.

Balsamic Strawberries

In a saucepan, combine the vinegar, brown sugar, and vanilla extract and reduce the liquid over medium-low heat to form a syrup. Add the strawberries while the liquid is still warm and toss to coat.

Strawberry Sauce

Purée the strawberries, granulated sugar, and lemon juice in a blender, then strain through a fine sieve.

To serve, ladle some strawberry sauce onto a plate. Place a meringue disc in the center and crack a small opening into the top of it. Scoop a dollop of whipped cream into the opening and top it with balsamic strawberries. Garnish with additional chopped walnuts if desired. Repeat with the remaining servings.

Serves 8

Pecan Tart

Tart Shell

7 tablespoons unsalted butter, chilled and cut into small cubes, plus more for the pan

6 tablespoons plus 2 teaspoons vegetable shortening

pinch salt

5 tablespoons plus 2 teaspoons granulated sugar

1 large egg

2 cups all-purpose flour

Confectioners' sugar, for sprinkling

Filling

3 tablespoons unsalted butter, softened

pinch salt

½ cup granulated sugar

3 large eggs

½ cup maple syrup

½ cup dark corn syrup

1 teaspoon vanilla extract

1¼ cups chopped pecans, toasted

Salted Caramel

Makes 4 cups

2¼ pounds granulated sugar

1½ teaspoons salt

9 tablespoons unsalted butter, cut into cubes

2 cups heavy cream

vanilla ice cream or whipped cream (page 178), for serving

Tart Shell

In a standing mixer, combine the butter, shortening, salt, and granulated sugar and mix until combined. Scrape the bowl, add the egg, and mix until combined. Scrape the bowl again and add the flour in two batches, scraping the bowl between each addition, and mix until smooth.

Form the dough into a disc, wrap it in plastic wrap, and refrigerate for at least 1 hour or up to 1 day.

Preheat the oven to 350°F.

Roll the dough into a 12-inch round and press it into a greased 9-inch tart pan with removable sides. Using a fork, poke holes all over the dough. Line with foil and fill with dried beans or pie weights.

Bake for 15 minutes, remove the weights, and bake for another 15 minutes until lightly golden. Let cool.

Filling

In a standing mixer on medium speed, cream together the butter, salt, and granulated sugar. Mix in the eggs one at a time, scraping the bowl after each addition. Reduce the speed to low and mix in the maple syrup, corn syrup, and vanilla until blended.

Line the cooled tart shell with the pecans and pour the filling over the pecans to cover. Bake for 35–45 minutes, until the filling is set around the edges but the center jiggles slightly. Let cool on wire rack for at least 1 hour for easier slicing.

Salted Caramel

In a pot with high walls, combine the granulated sugar, salt, and enough water to give the sugar a wet sand texture. Wipe out any sugar clinging to the sides of the pot, cover with plastic wrap, and cook over medium-high heat until the sugar approaches an amber color, about 20 minutes. Remove the pan from the heat and very carefully whisk in the butter and cream (the caramel will bubble and steam so it's best to whisk in a little at a time).

To serve, remove the sides of the tart pan and slice the tart into eight equal slices. Serve warm with the salted caramel sauce, vanilla ice cream or whipped cream, and a dash of confectioners' sugar.

Serves 6

Blueberry Crisp

Streusel Topping

Makes 2 cups

½ cup all-purpose flour

½ cup whole wheat flour

½ cup (1 stick) unsalted butter, cut into small pieces

½ cup packed light brown sugar

¾ teaspoon ground cinnamon

Blueberry Filling

6 cups fresh blueberries

1 tablespoon cornstarch

¼ cup packed light brown sugar

¼ teaspoon ground nutmeg

Raspberry Sauce (optional)

Makes 3 cups

4 pints fresh raspberries

½ cup granulated sugar

2 tablespoons fresh lemon juice

Streusel Topping

Place both flours, the butter, brown sugar, and cinnamon in the bowl of a food processor and pulse until the mixture resembles a coarse meal.

Blueberry Filling

Preheat the oven to 375°F.

Toss the blueberries with the cornstarch, brown sugar, and nutmeg and transfer to a baking dish or four individual baking dishes. Evenly sprinkle the streusel on top and bake for 40 minutes, until the topping is golden brown and the filling is bubbling.

Raspberry Sauce

If you're making the raspberry sauce, combine the raspberries, granulated sugar, and lemon juice in a saucepan and simmer for 10 minutes. Carefully transfer to a blender and purée until smooth. Strain the sauce through a fine sieve to remove the seeds. Let chill in the refrigerator for 2 hours or overnight.

Serve the crisp immediately or rewarm it in an oven or broiler. Serve the raspberry sauce on the side, if using.

White Chocolate Mousse Cake

9 ounces chocolate wafers

6 tablespoons melted butter

16 ounces white chocolate

3 large eggs, separated

pinch salt

½ cup sugar

3 cups heavy cream, 2½ cups whipped to soft peaks

2 tablespoons white crème de cacao

Raspberry Sauce (page 182)

Preheat the oven to 350°F. Liberally spray the bottom and sides of a 10-inch springform pan with baking spray.

In a food processor, pulse the chocolate wafers until the crumbs are very fine, then place the crumbs in a bowl with the butter and stir to combine. Firmly press about two-thirds of the crumbs onto the sides of the pan and the remaining crumbs on the bottom of the pan (use the bottom of a drinking glass to create an even layer).

Bake the crust for 5 minutes. Allow to cool completely or freeze for later use.

Melt the white chocolate in a double boiler until it reaches a temperature of 130°F, stirring occasionally until completely smooth. Set aside and keep warm.

Put the egg whites in a standing mixer, add a pinch of salt, and beat until frothy. With the mixer running, gradually add the sugar to the egg whites and beat until the mixture holds stiff, glossy peaks. Set aside.

Put the egg yolks in a large bowl, whisk in the ½ cup of unwhipped heavy cream, add the melted white chocolate, and stir well to combine. Whisk in the crème de cacao until the mixture is smooth. Gently fold in the beaten egg whites until well combined. Fold in the 2½ cups of whipped cream, stir well to combine, and pour the filling into the prepared crust.

Freeze until firm, at least 4 hours or overnight.

To serve, remove the cake from the freezer and release from the pan. Cut the cake into wedges, transfer to plates, and spoon the raspberry sauce onto the plates or over the slices of cake.

Maple Crème Brûlée

8 large egg yolks

1 cup granulated sugar

½ vanilla bean

¾ cup maple syrup

1 quart heavy cream

superfine white sugar, for sprinkling

What sets our crème brûlée apart from any other? In Vermont, we are fortunate to avail ourselves of local heavy cream so thick you have to use a knife to get it to start pouring from the bottle it comes in. In this simple and straightforward recipe, we prepare the brûlée in individual ramekins rather than in one large baking dish. The number of servings will depend on the size of the ramekins.

In a bowl, mix the egg yolks and granulated sugar with a whisk until the mixture is light yellow. With the tip of a sharp knife, slice the vanilla bean in half and scrape the seeds into the yolk mixture. Stir in the maple syrup and heavy cream and mix thoroughly. Chill for at least 4 hours, or up to a day.

Preheat the oven to 350°F.

Pour the custard into four to six ramekins. Bake them in a hot water bath in the middle of the oven for about 45 minutes, or until a knife inserted into a custard comes out clean. Remove from the water bath and let cool completely. May refrigerate for several hours or up to several days at this point.

Just before serving, sprinkle superfine sugar evenly over the custards. Use a kitchen blowtorch, or set under a preheated broiler (watching carefully), to caramelize the sugar. Let stand for 3 to 5 minutes, or until the sugar is hardened, then serve.

Chocolate Bombs with Cherry Compote

1 pound bittersweet chocolate

12 ounces (3 sticks) unsalted butter

1 cup plus 6 tablespoons packed brown sugar

7 tablespoons all-purpose flour

2 teaspoons salt

7 large eggs

1 tablespoon vanilla extract

granulated sugar, for coating ramekins

Cherry Compote

1 cup dried cherries

¼ cup orange juice

vanilla ice cream, for serving

In a double boiler, melt the chocolate and butter, stirring occasionally, until smooth, then remove from the heat.

In a standing mixer with a paddle attachment, combine the brown sugar, flour, and salt and mix to combine, breaking up any clumps of sugar.

In a 2-cup pitcher, crack the eggs, add the vanilla, and whisk to combine. Add the beaten eggs to the sugar mixture in three stages, mixing until incorporated and smooth. When all the eggs are added, slowly whisk in the chocolate mixture, then transfer the batter to a container and refrigerate for at least 2 hours, or overnight.

Preheat the oven to 325°F.

Spray eight 4-ounce ramekins or foil cups with cooking spray and coat with granulated sugar. Divide the batter evenly among the ramekins. Bake for about 30 minutes, until the cakes have risen slightly but are still slightly gooey in the center.

Cherry Compote

Combine the cherries and orange juice in a pot. Simmer for 10 minutes.

To serve, place a chocolate bomb on a plate, spoon a generous portion of cherry compote on top, and add a scoop of vanilla ice cream on the side.

ACKNOWLEDGMENTS

Pia Pearce

Alone we go fast, together we go far!

This revised and expanded edition of *A Way of Living* has truly been a team effort in the best sense of the word. Leading us in this achievement is our good friend Glenn Suokko, a designer, photographer, writer, and artist, who also oversees the Art Gallery at Simon Pearce in Quechee, Vermont. Simon and I thank Glenn for his new photography, editorial direction, and graphic design of this book.

Special thanks to Jerod Rockwell, our restaurant director, and Jeremy Conway, executive chef, for the many hours they spent in developing the recipes, testing them, and in preparing the food for photography. We also appreciate how much they continually strive to provide exceptional food and service for the guests who dine at our restaurant in Quechee.

Offering recipes that started in our restaurant and adapting them for the home cook demanded that we test and retest them in order to make sure they are just right. Grateful appreciation is due to our dedicated testers: Rose Dulac, Christine Geisler, Marie Holzwarth-Reidman, Deb Ivy, Wendy Jackson, Pam Lessard, Meg Mahoney, James Murray, Adam and Kyla Pearce, Phoebe Preston, Heidi Reidman, Lisa Rosse, and Dana Sabatino.

Other essential assistance has come from Deb Ivy, vice president of brand experience at Simon Pearce, for coordinating this project and keeping us organized and on track; from Pam Lessard for deftly coordinating the glass and pottery for numerous photo shoots; from my good friend Ruth Stiff for editorial support; from Karen Gansz for coming to the rescue on a moments' notice whenever necessary; from Carol Magadini for providing floral arrangements; and from Sarah Scheffel for copyediting and proofreading the recipes and essay texts.

Simon and I are truly grateful to Jay Benson, chief executive officer, and to everyone who has played a part in making this revised edition possible. We are astounded by how far we have come over the course of forty years, and well understand that it's the teamwork of so many that has made it all possible.

Simon Pearce
109 Park Road
Windsor, Vermont 05089
802 674 6280

simonpearce.com
800 774 5277

REVISED AND EXPANDED EDITION
ISBN 978-0-615-30627-8

Library of Congress Control Number: 2009931763

Photography and design by Glenn Suokko

Copyediting by Sarah Scheffel

Printed in the United States of America by Puritan Capital

About the book:

This revised and expanded edition of *A Way of Living* celebrates what's changed and what's new in Pia and Simon Pearce's lives and work over the last ten years. The book introduces their growing family, takes the reader into their home and around their table, into their glass and pottery workshops, and behind the scenes where the chefs from the Simon Pearce restaurant have prepared delicious new recipes. To Pia and Simon, living simply with beautiful things, creating imaginative table settings with glass and pottery, and cooking good food with fresh ingredients go hand-in-hand in creating their way of living.

About the authors:

Pia McDonnell Pearce earned a master's degree in human development and an EdD in educational organization and leadership before moving to Ireland in 1978 to live with Simon. They were married in New Jersey in 1979 and decided to move their growing glass business to Vermont in 1981. Soon after moving to Quechee, their family expanded through the addition of four sons. While very much a hands-on mother, Pia also spent time developing the mail-order business for Simon Pearce Glass and opened what has become the flagship store in Quechee, Vermont. Given a life-long interest in good food, she helped Simon establish the Simon Pearce restaurant in 1984. Over the past forty years, Pia has continued to support the success of the company as well as pursue her work in educational advocacy with a special focus on people with Down syndrome and learning differences. She is currently a member of the board of directors of Simon Pearce, and serves as the president of the LoveYourBrain Foundation, a nonprofit organization that offers programs designed for people with traumatic brain injuries and their caregivers.

Simon Pearce started his early creative life as a potter at Shanagarry Pottery, his family's business in County Cork, on the southeastern coast of Ireland. He trained as a glassblower at Glasfabriek Leerdam in the Netherlands, Venini glassworks in Italy, and Orrefors in Sweden. Simon established his glass business in Bennettsbridge, Ireland, in the mid-1970s. He moved to the United States in 1981, settling in Vermont, to pursue his dream of creating handcrafted utilitarian glass using old-world techniques and the finest raw materials. He and his wife, Pia McDonnell Pearce, created Simon Pearce Glass. For nearly forty years, Simon Pearce's glassware has been famous for its range of styles, pure materials, and luminosity.

Glenn Suokko authored, photographed, and designed *Shelburne Farms: House, Gardens, Farm, and Barns* (Rizzoli, 2017) and *Simon Pearce: Design for Living* (Rizzoli, 2016). He is coauthor, photographer, and designer of *A Way of Living* (Simon Pearce, 2009 and 2019) and *Pastoral* (2005–12). He is editor of *A New Pastoral*, a quarterly journal dedicated to featuring home-cooking recipes and stories from Vermont. He also oversees the Art Gallery at Simon Pearce in Quechee, Vermont, where he shows his paintings as well as the work of artists from the region.